STORIES OF THE OLD TESTAMENT COLORING BOOK

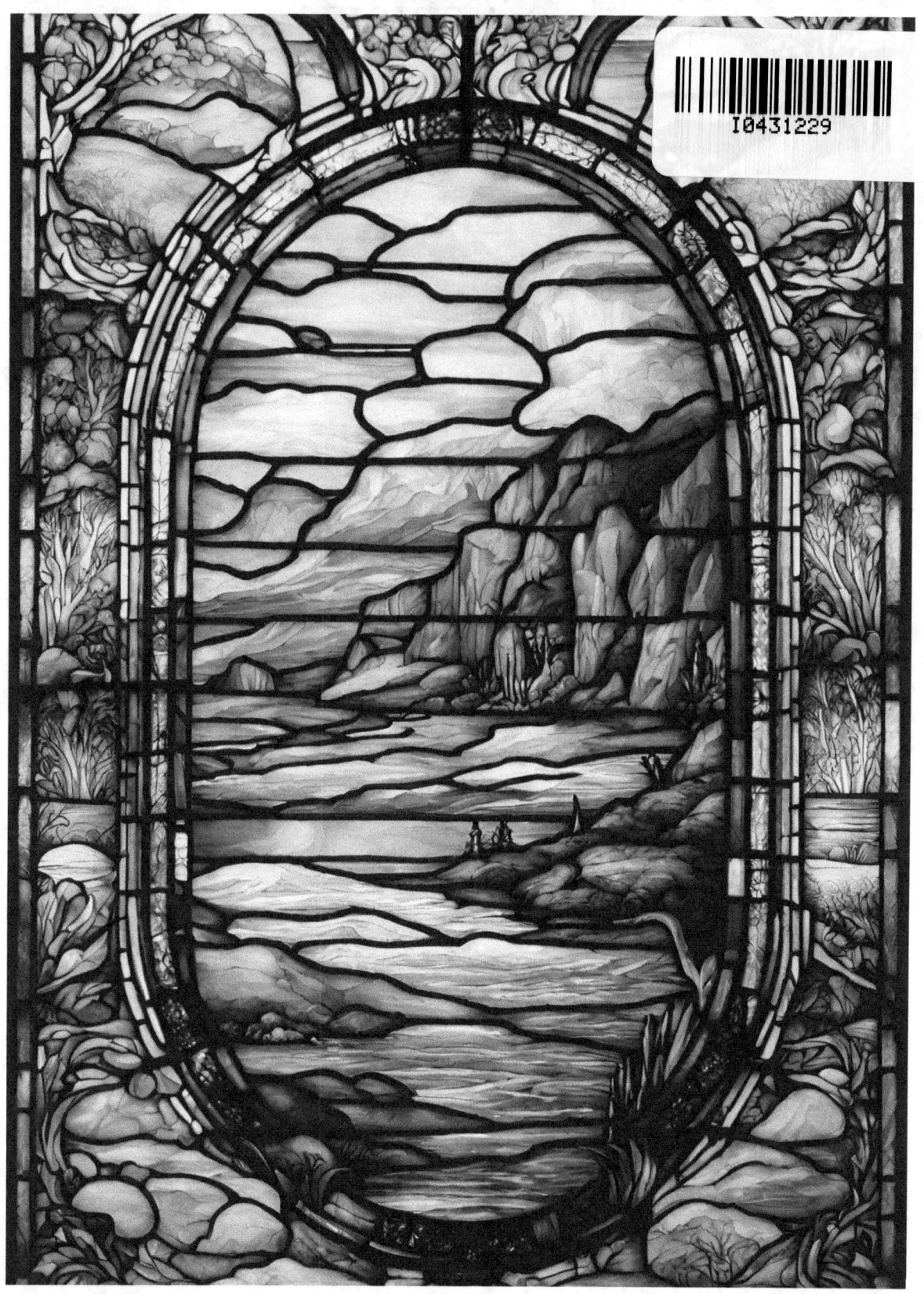

Table of Contents

GARDEN OF EDEN...1

TREE OF LIFE..2

THE SERPENT..3

FRUIT OF TEMPTATION..4

FIERY SWORD OF EDEN'S ENTRY....................................5

THE FLOOD & NOAH'S ARK...6

ANIMALS RELEASED TO NEW LAND................................7

THE TOWER OF BABEL...8

ABRAHAM LOOKING AT THE STARS................................9

JACOB & ESAU...10

JACOB'S ALDDER VISION..11

JOSEPH AND HIS ELEVN BROTHERS..............................12

THE BURNING BUSH..13

THE PLAGUE OF FROGS..14

THE FIRST PASSOVER...15

EXODUS FROM EGYPT..16

PILLAR OF FIRE...17

PARTING OF THE RED SEA...18

THE TEN COMMANDMENTS..19

ANCIENT CITY OF JERICHO..20

ANCIENT MOUNTAINS OF MOAB..................................21

SAMSON FIGHTING THE PHILISTINES..........................22

THE DEA SEA...23

ANCIENT BABYLON...24

DANIEL & THE LIONS DEN..25

ANCIENT SAMARIA...26

VISIONS OF CHERUBIM..27

THE GREAT FISH OF JONAH...28

ANCIENT NINEVAH...29

THE LION OF JUDAH...30

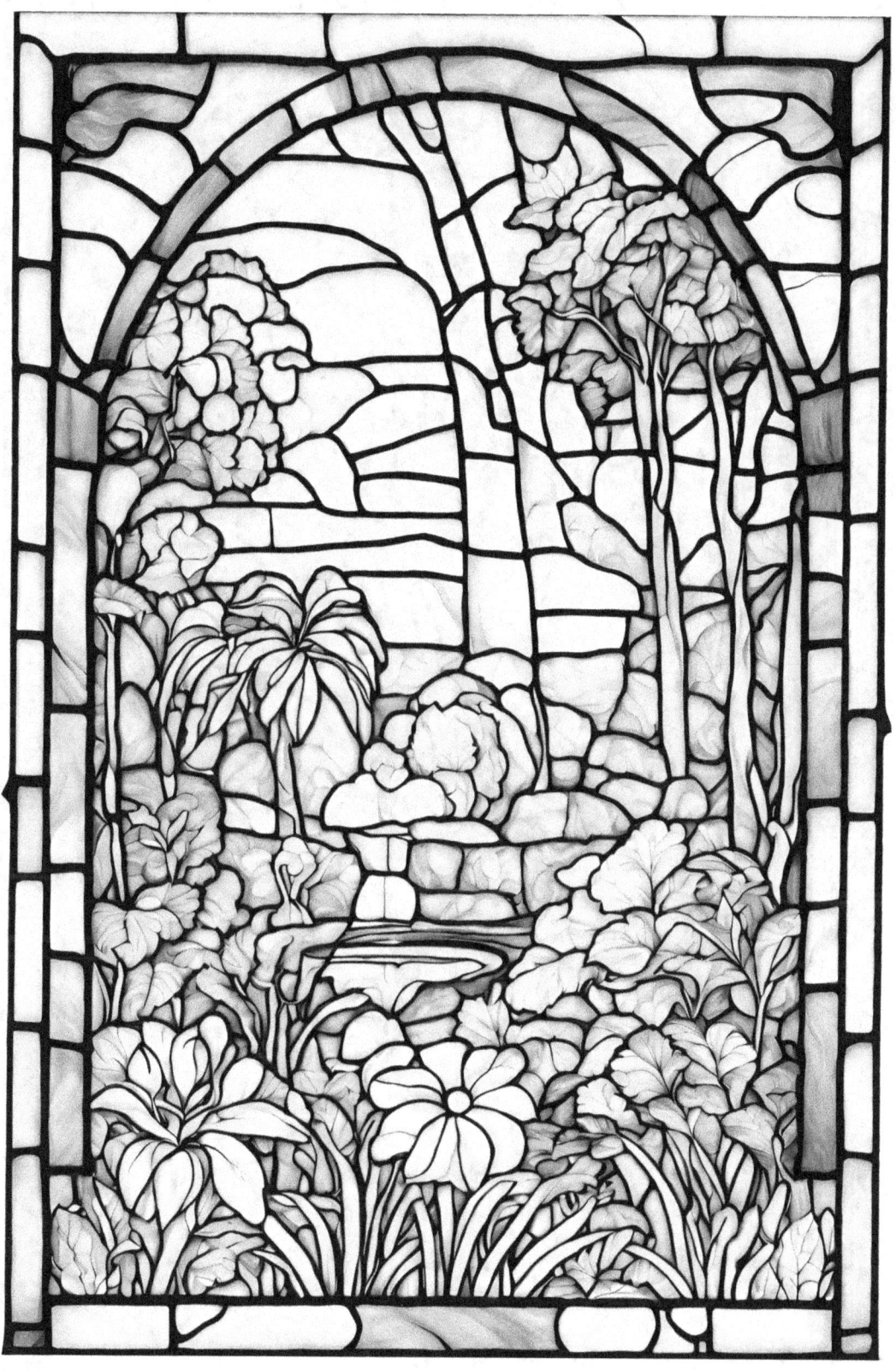

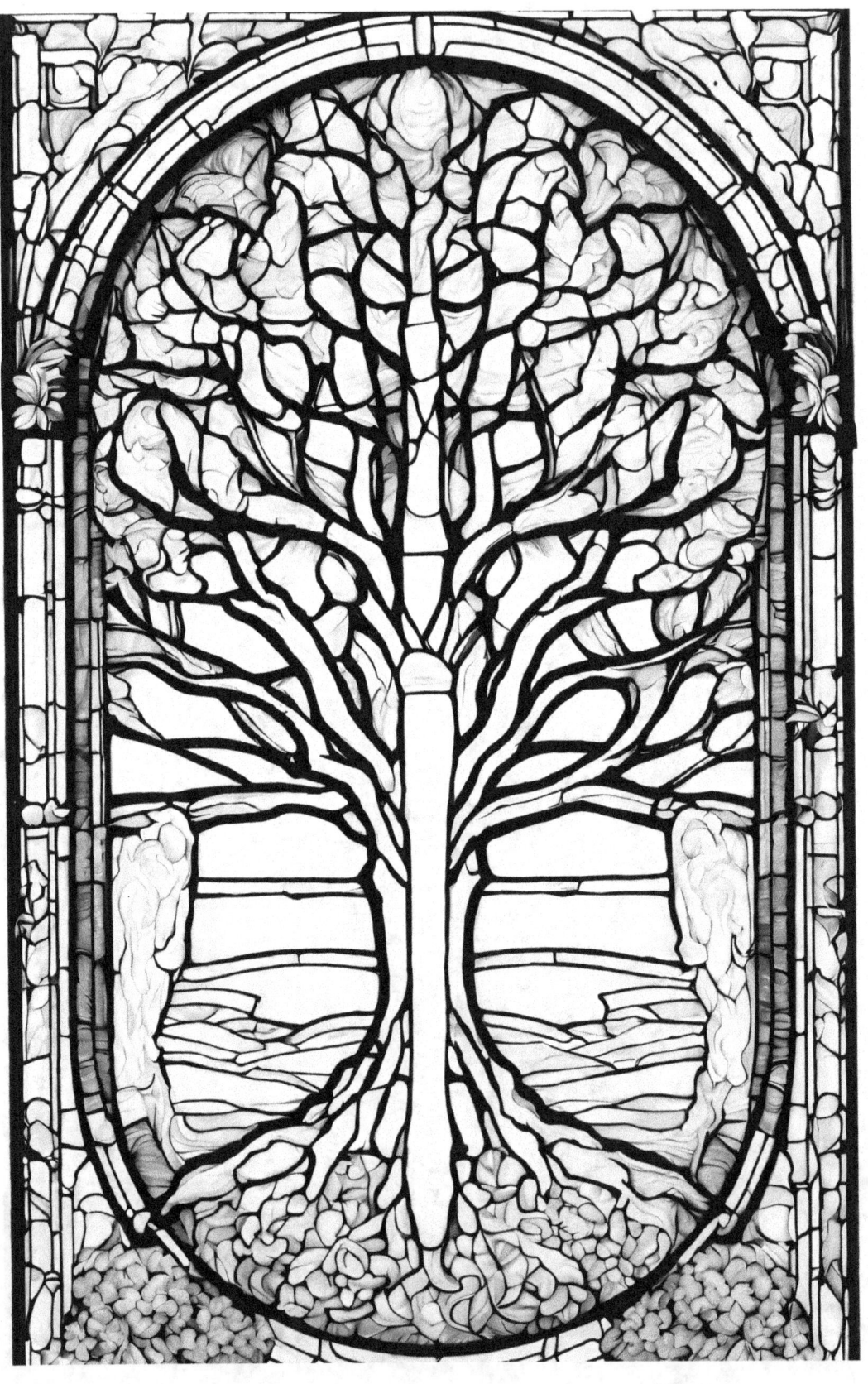

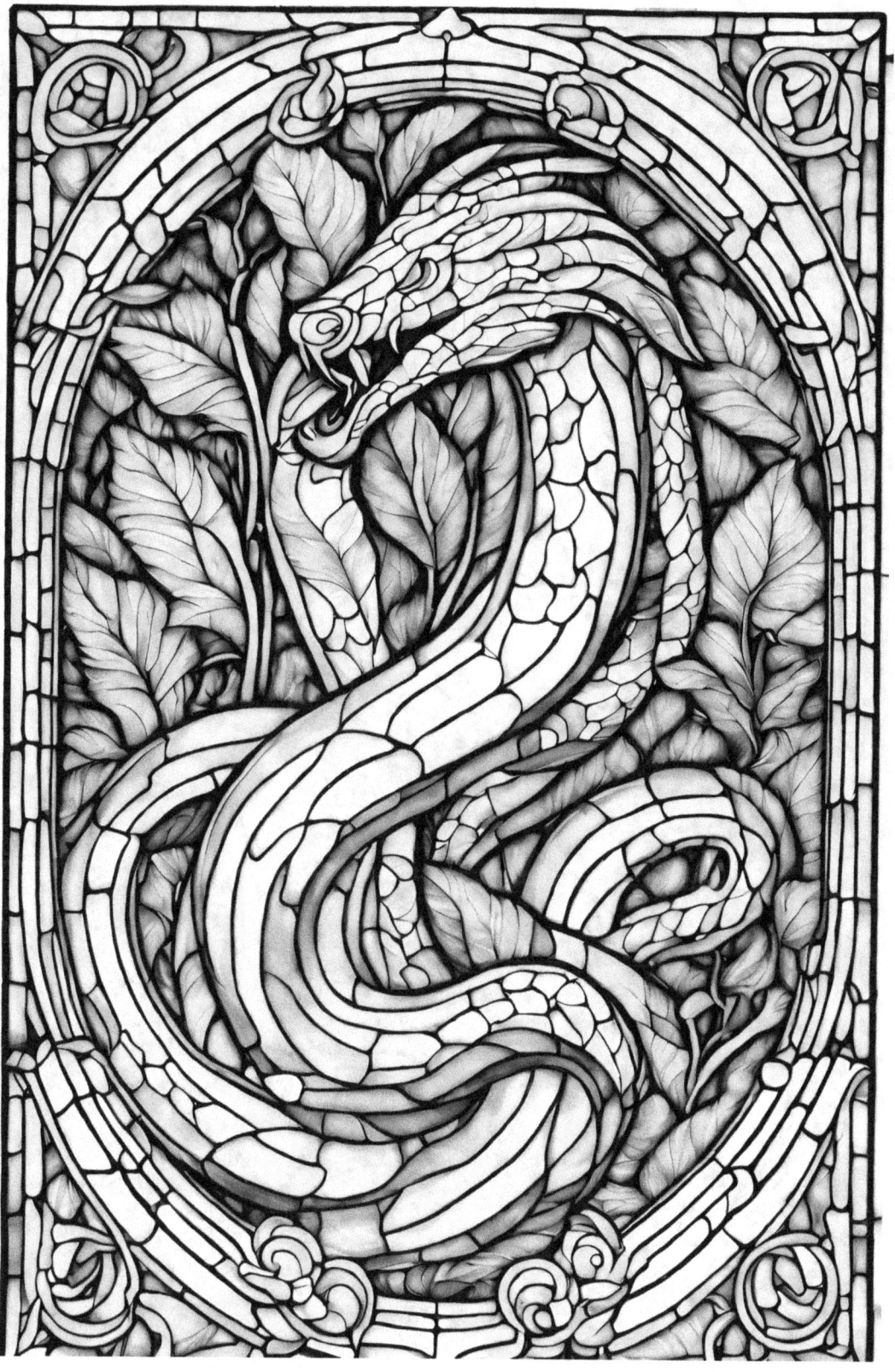

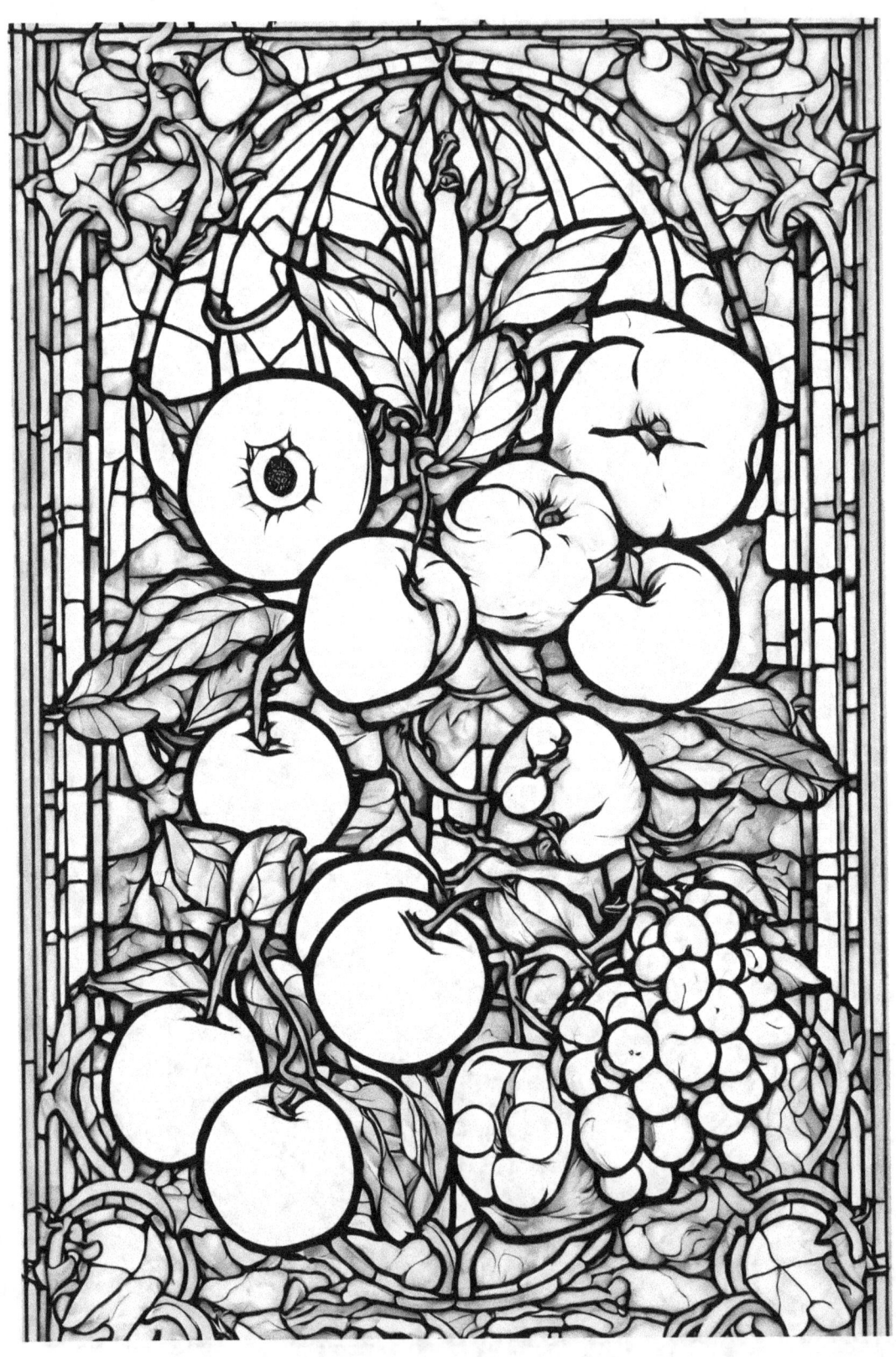

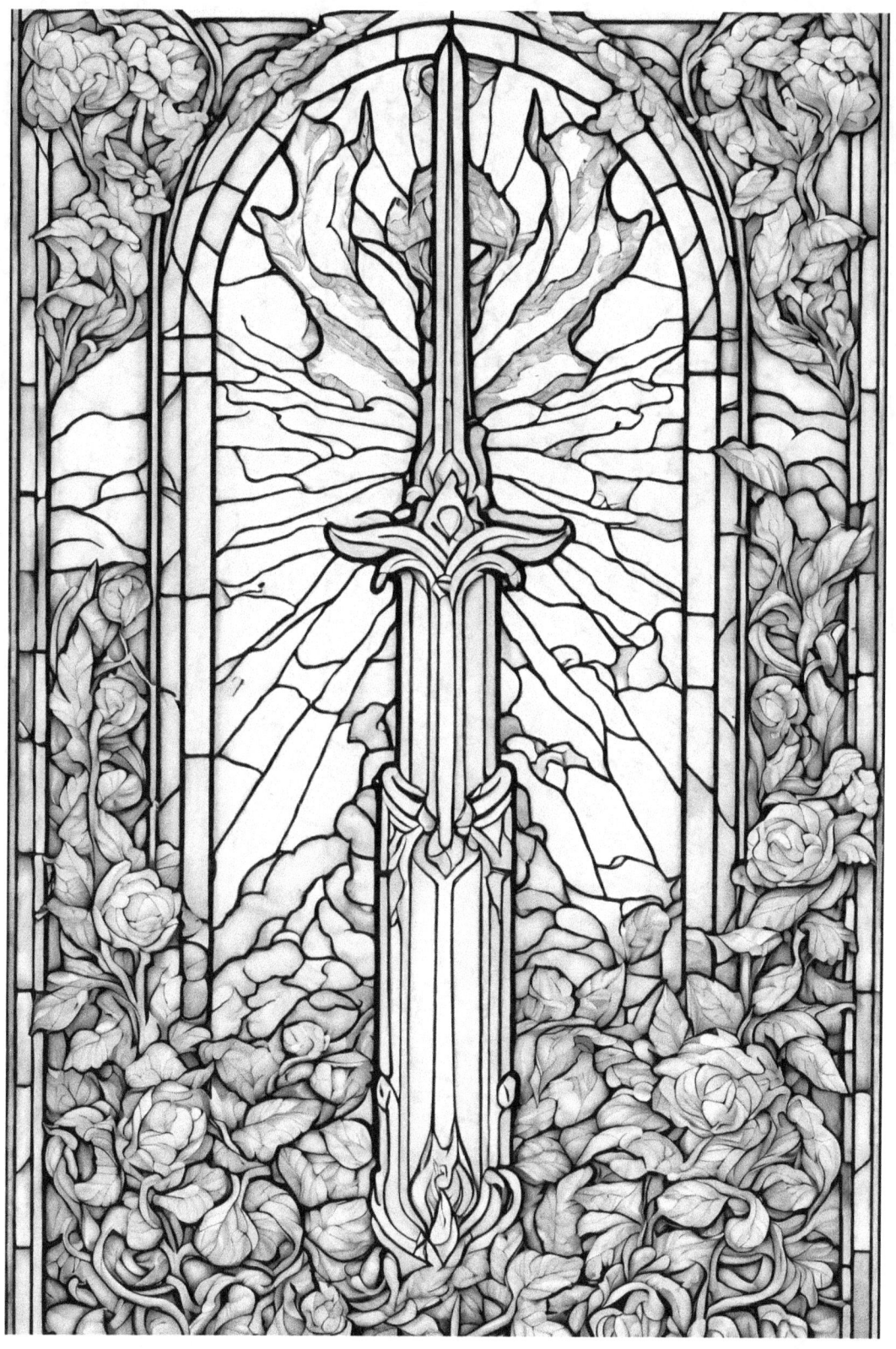

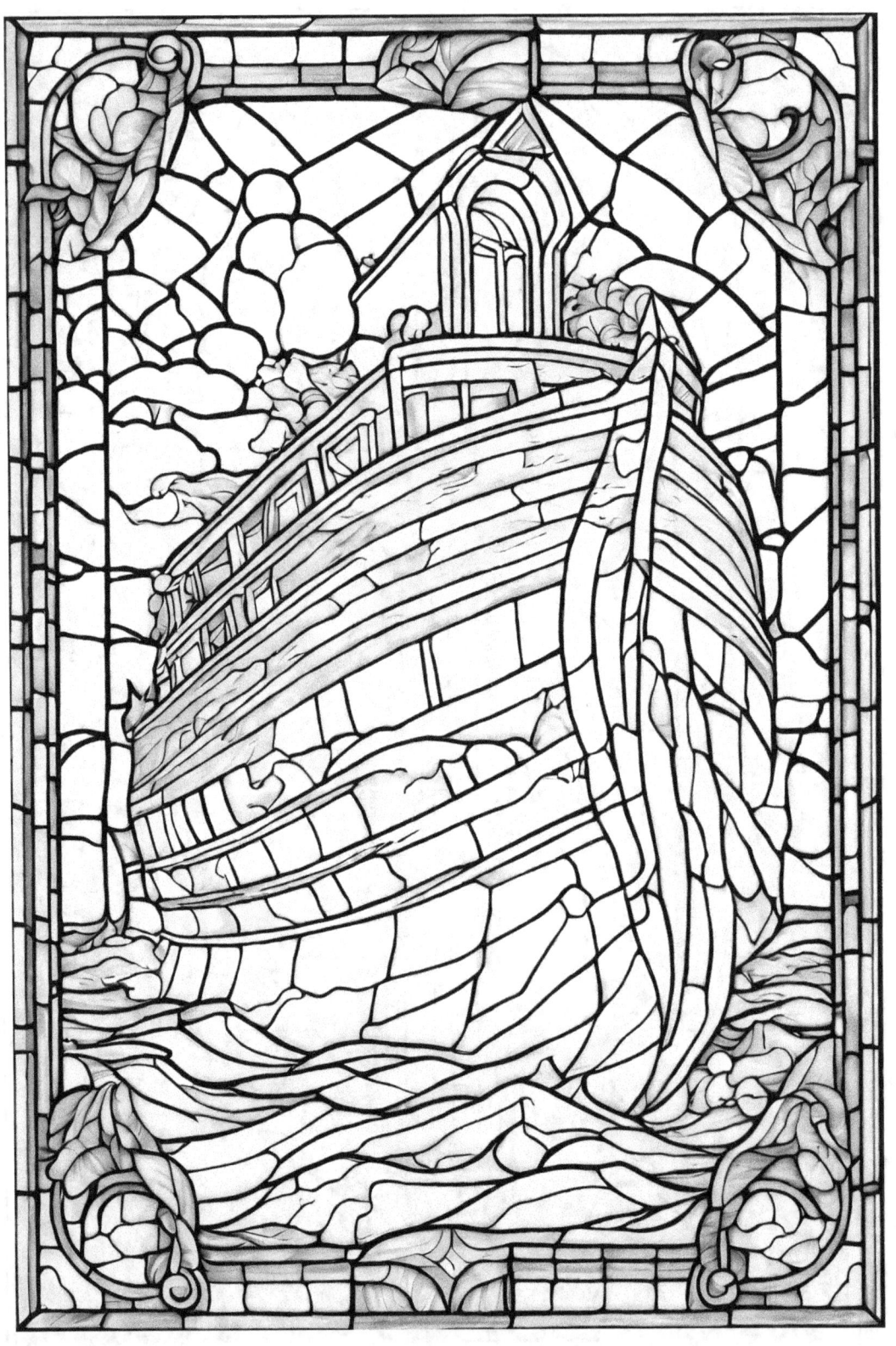

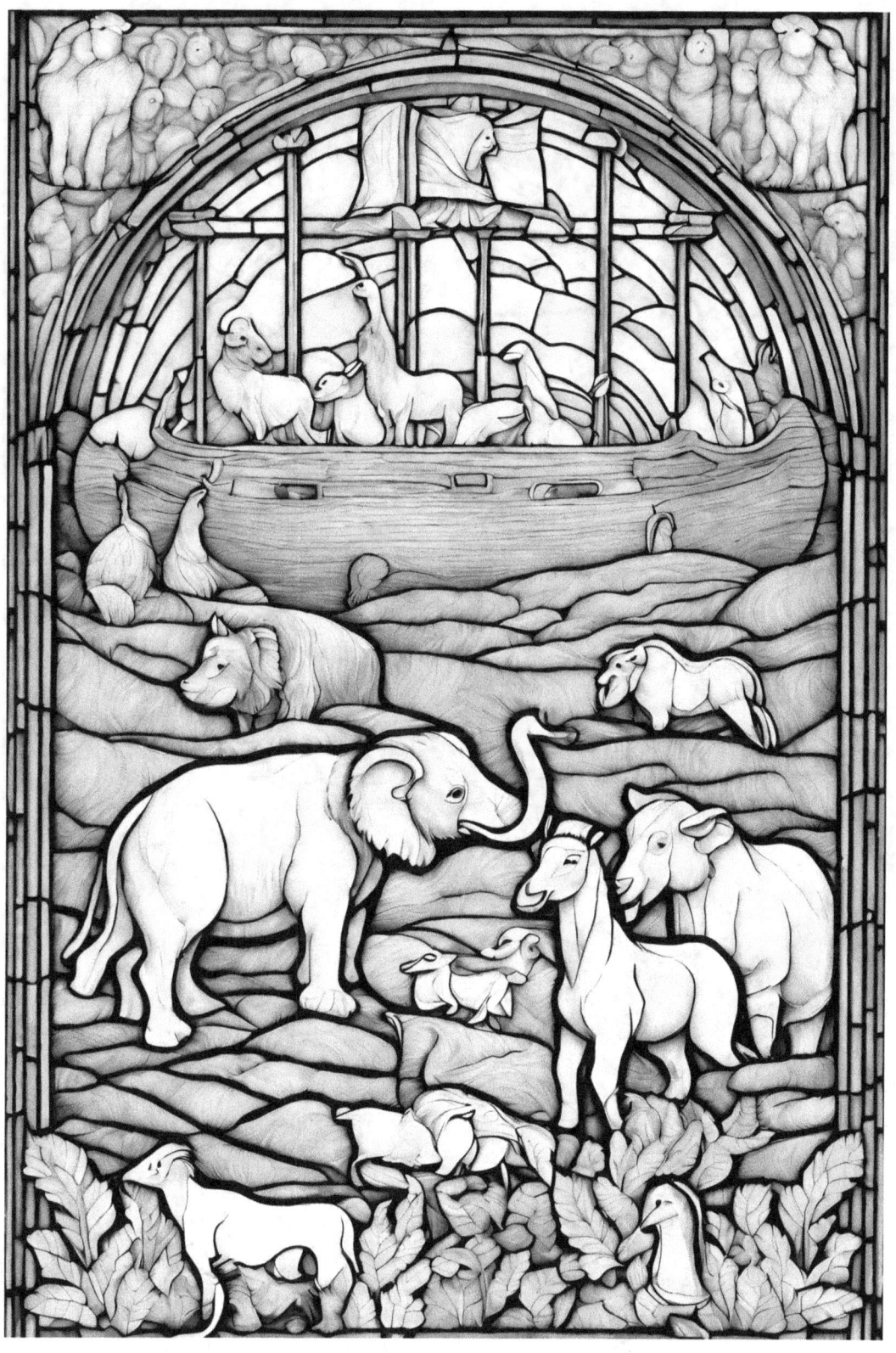

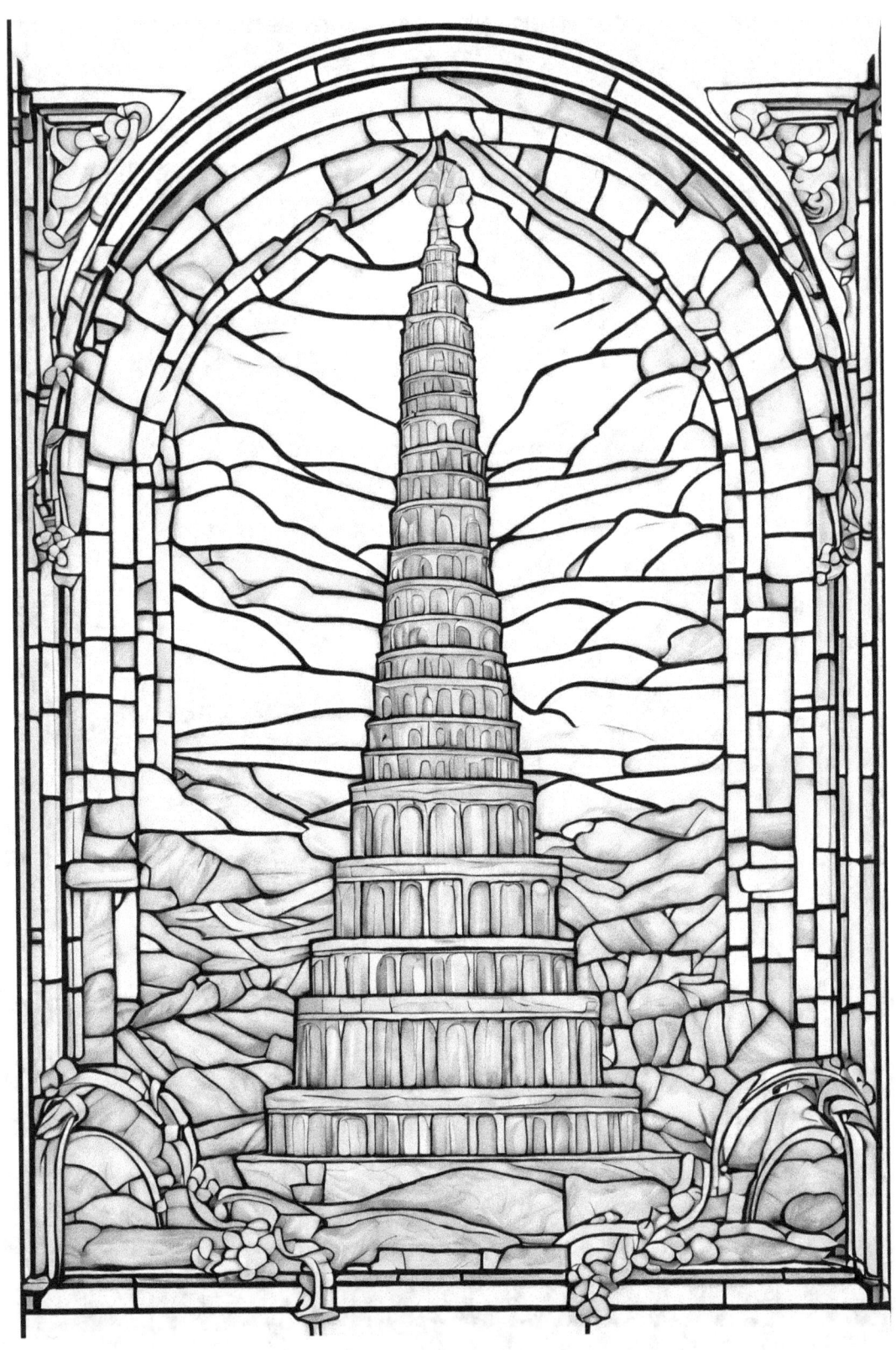

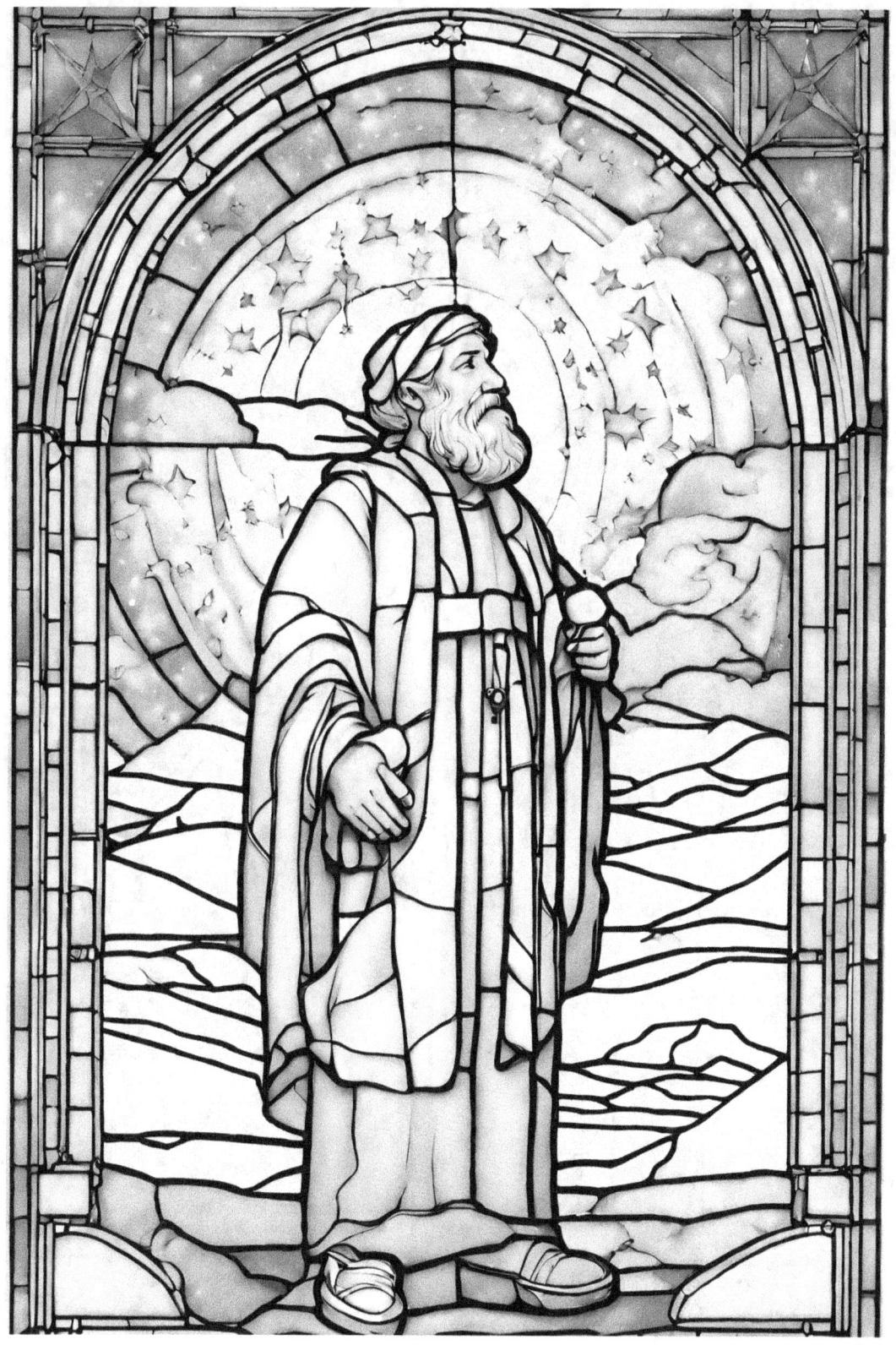

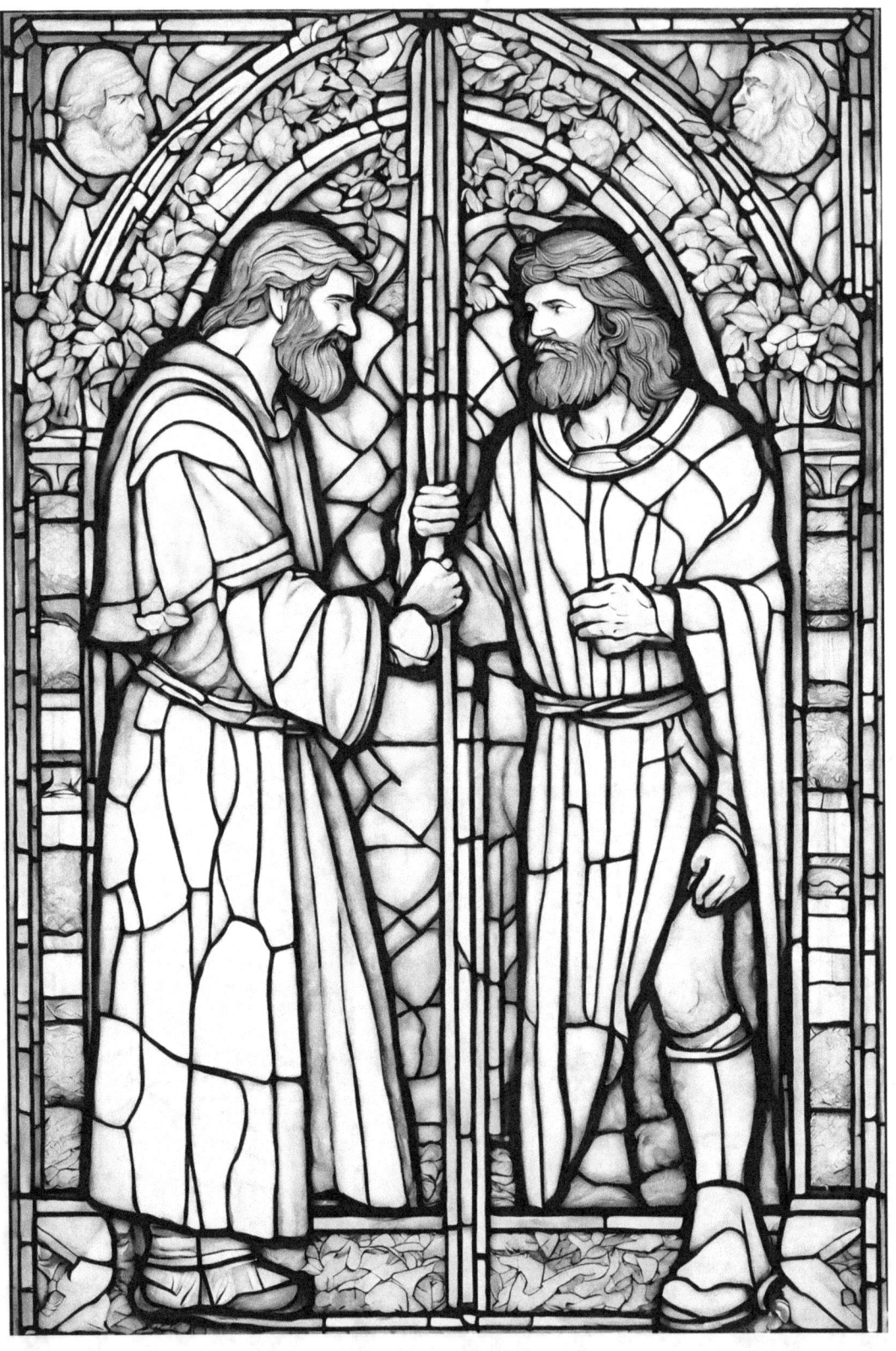

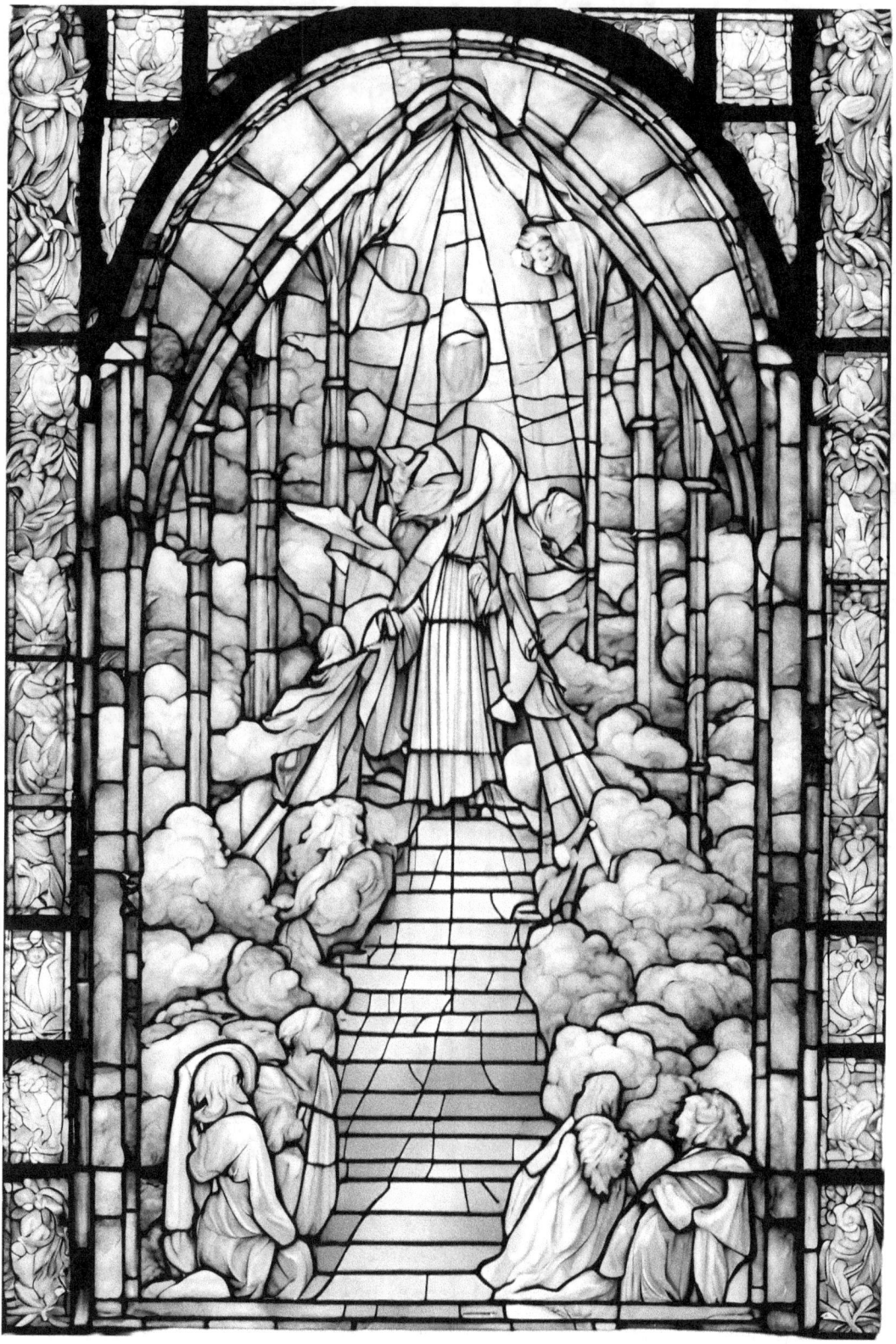

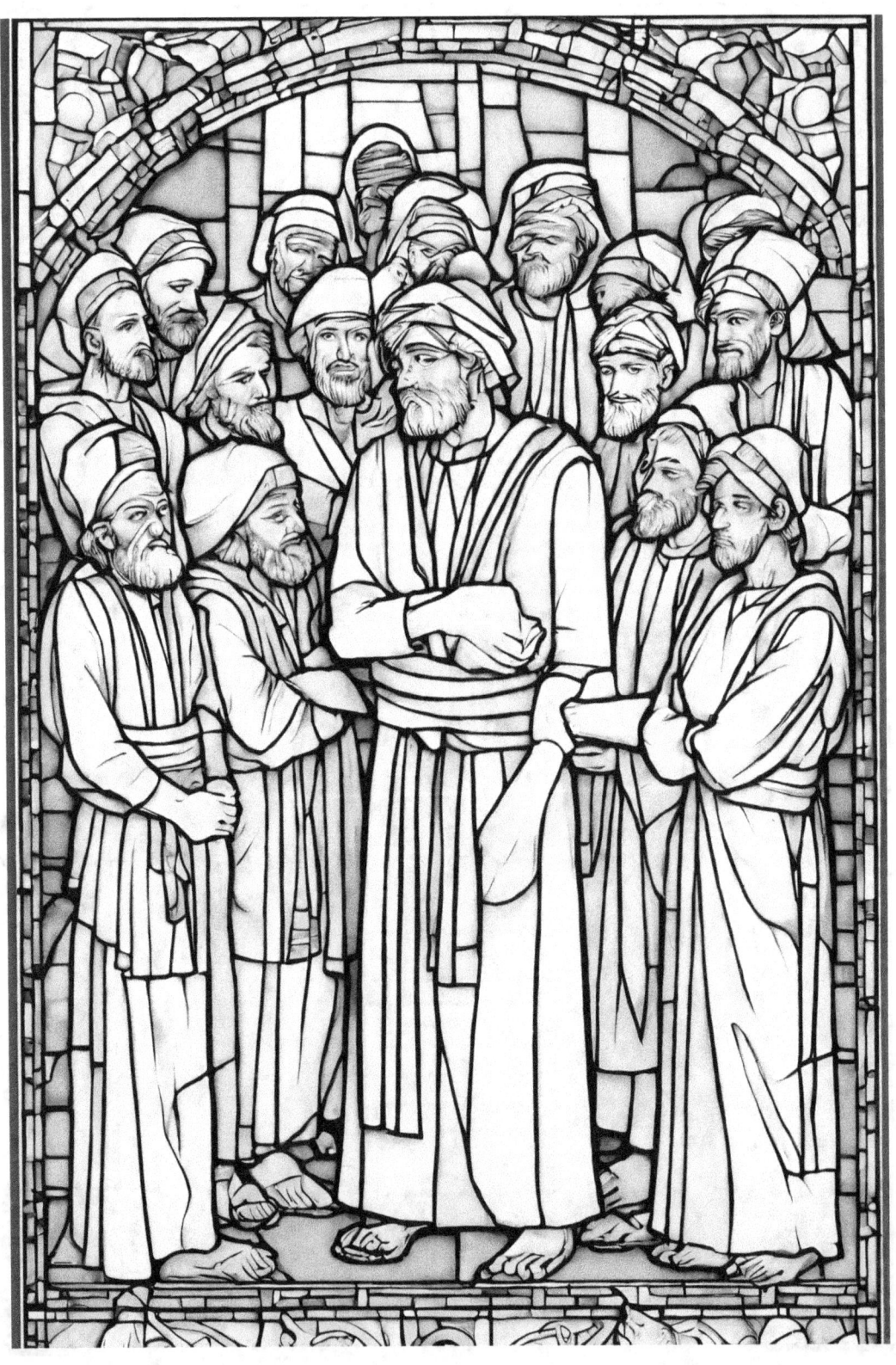

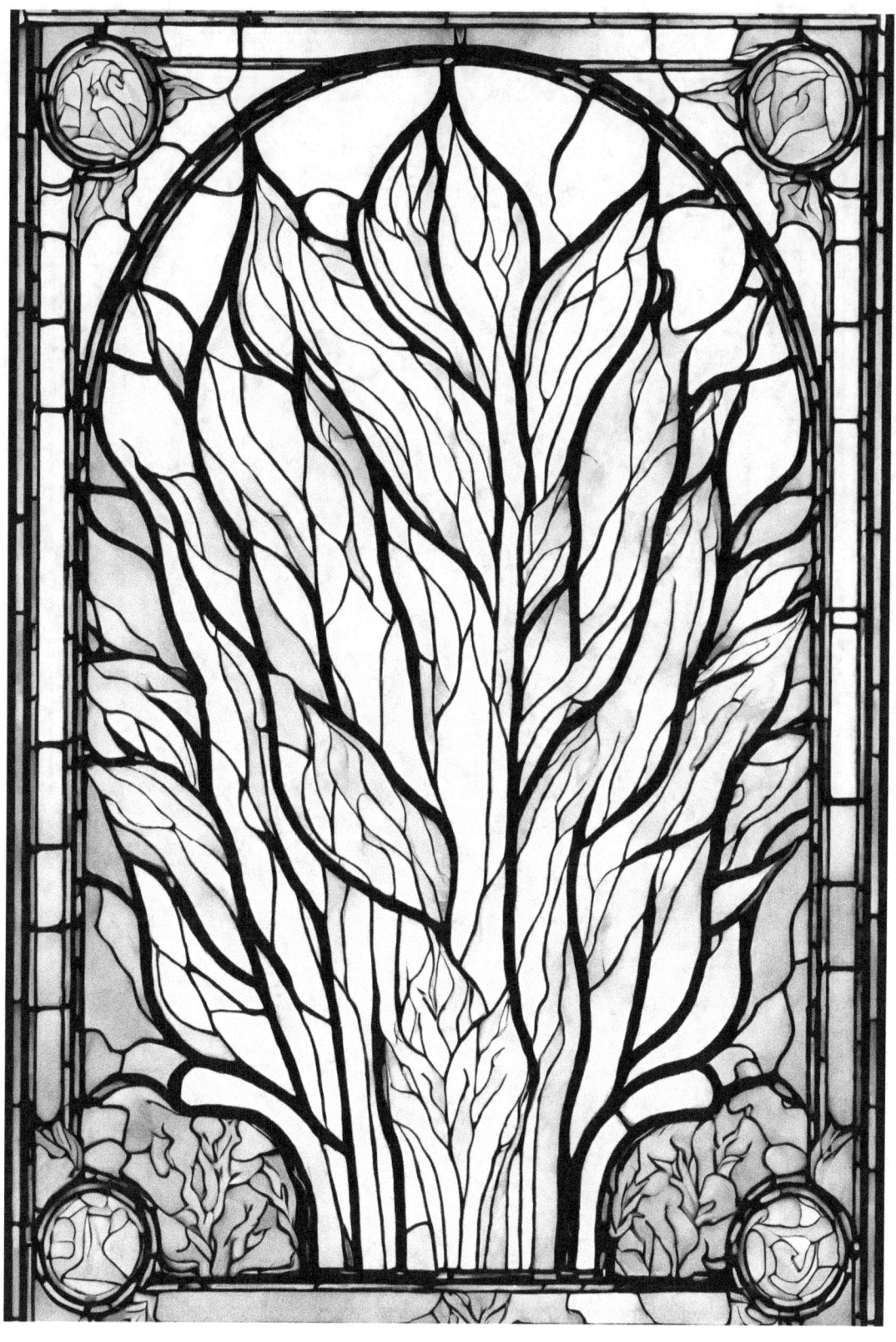

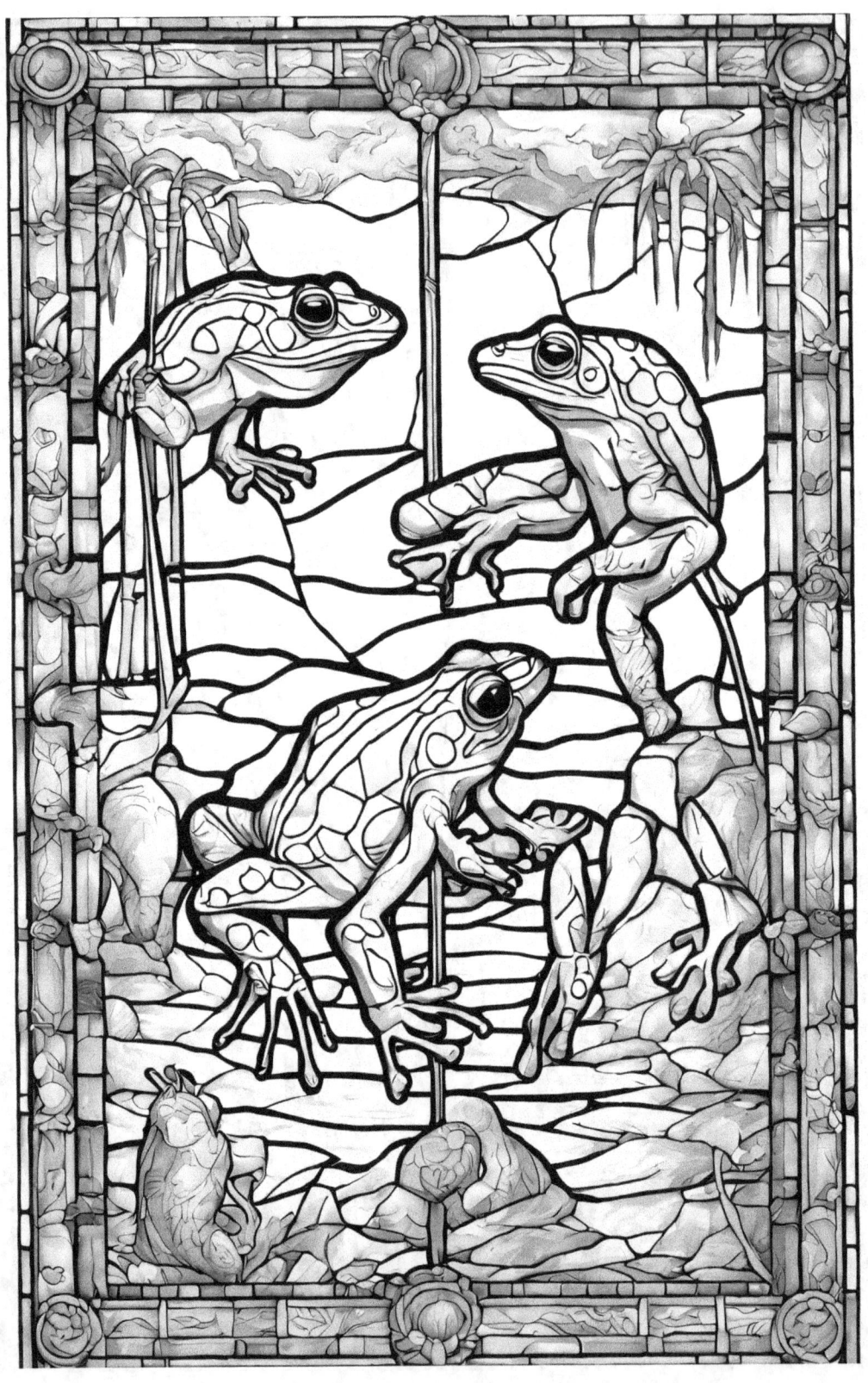

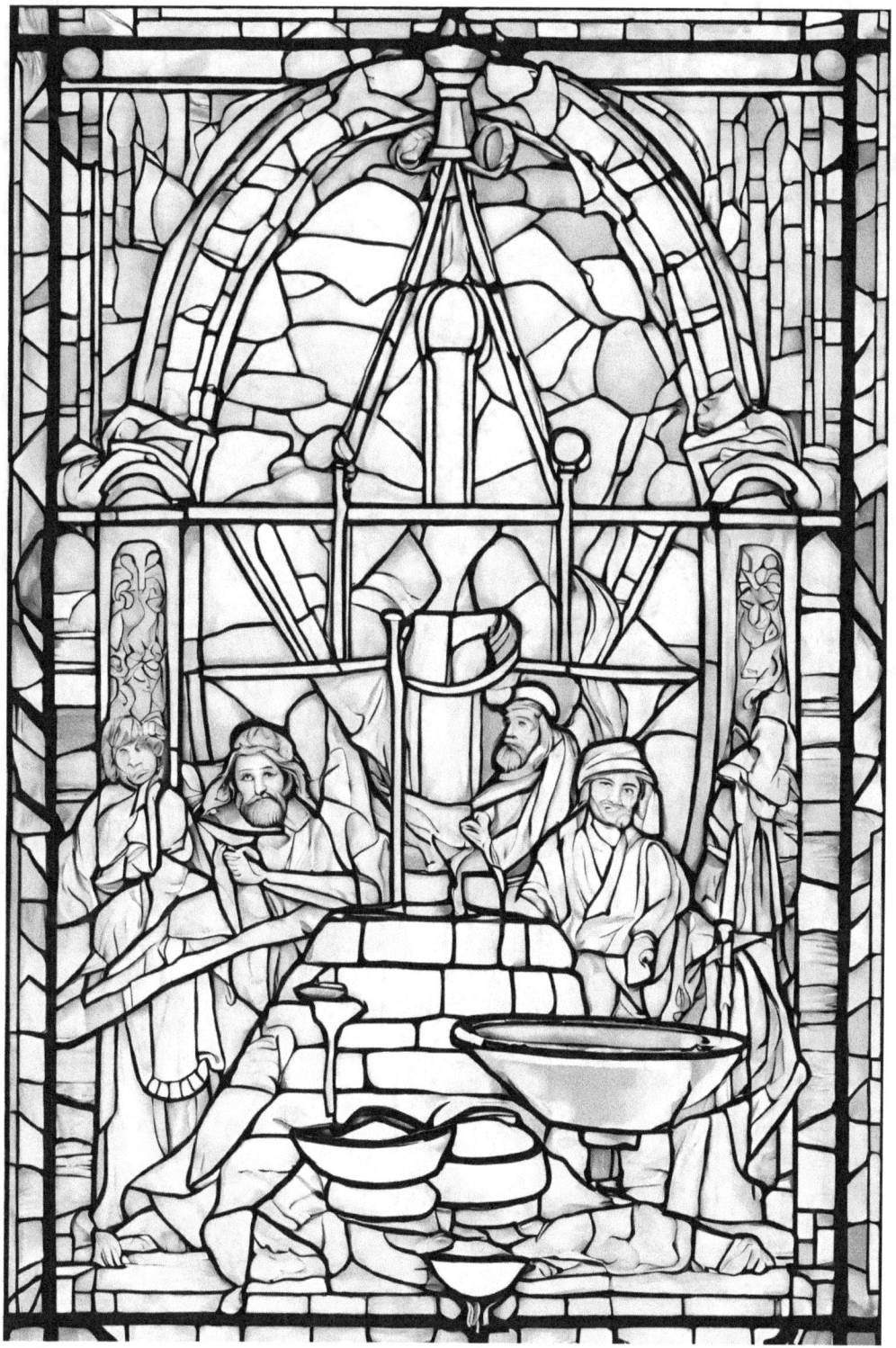

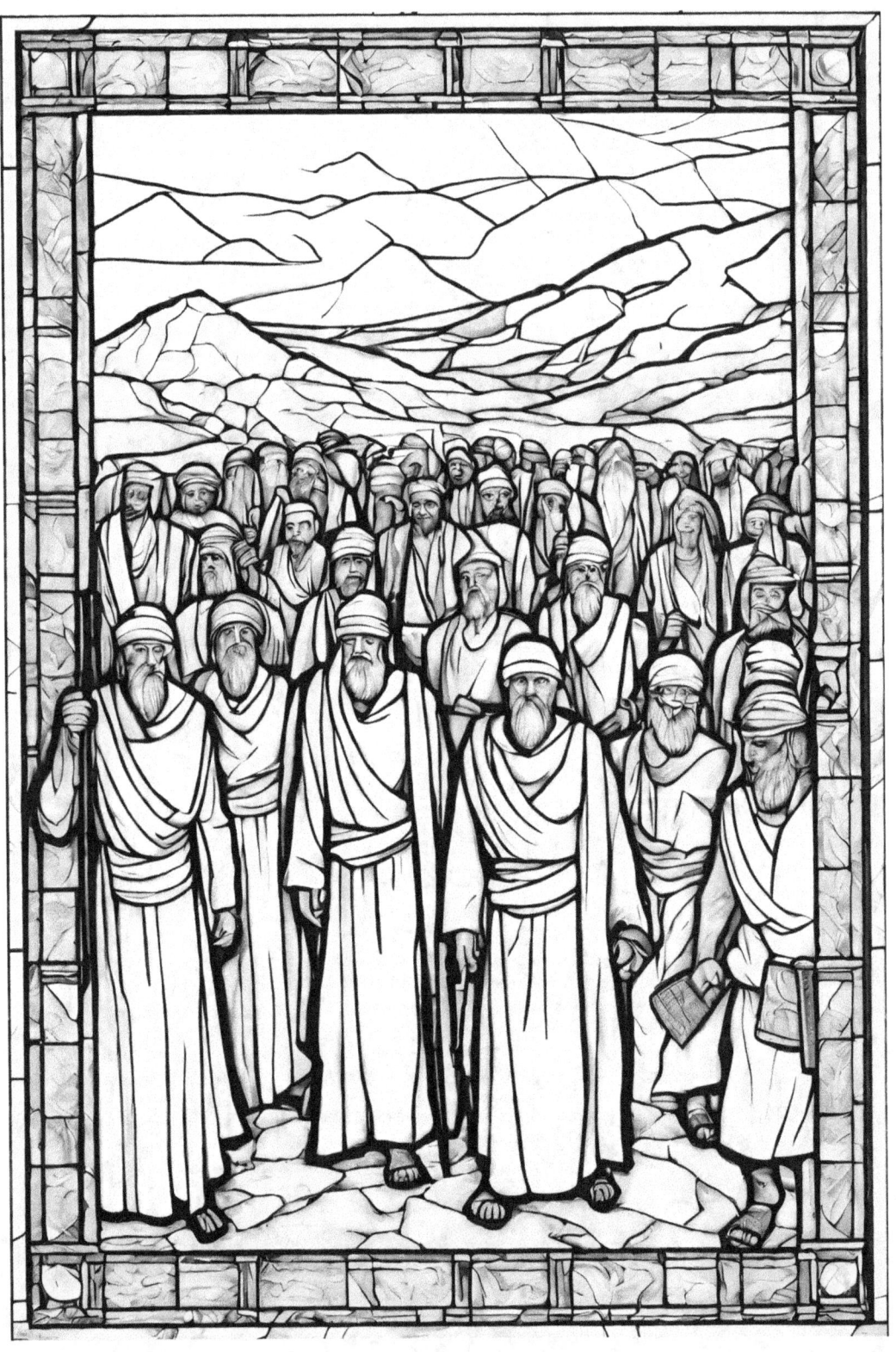

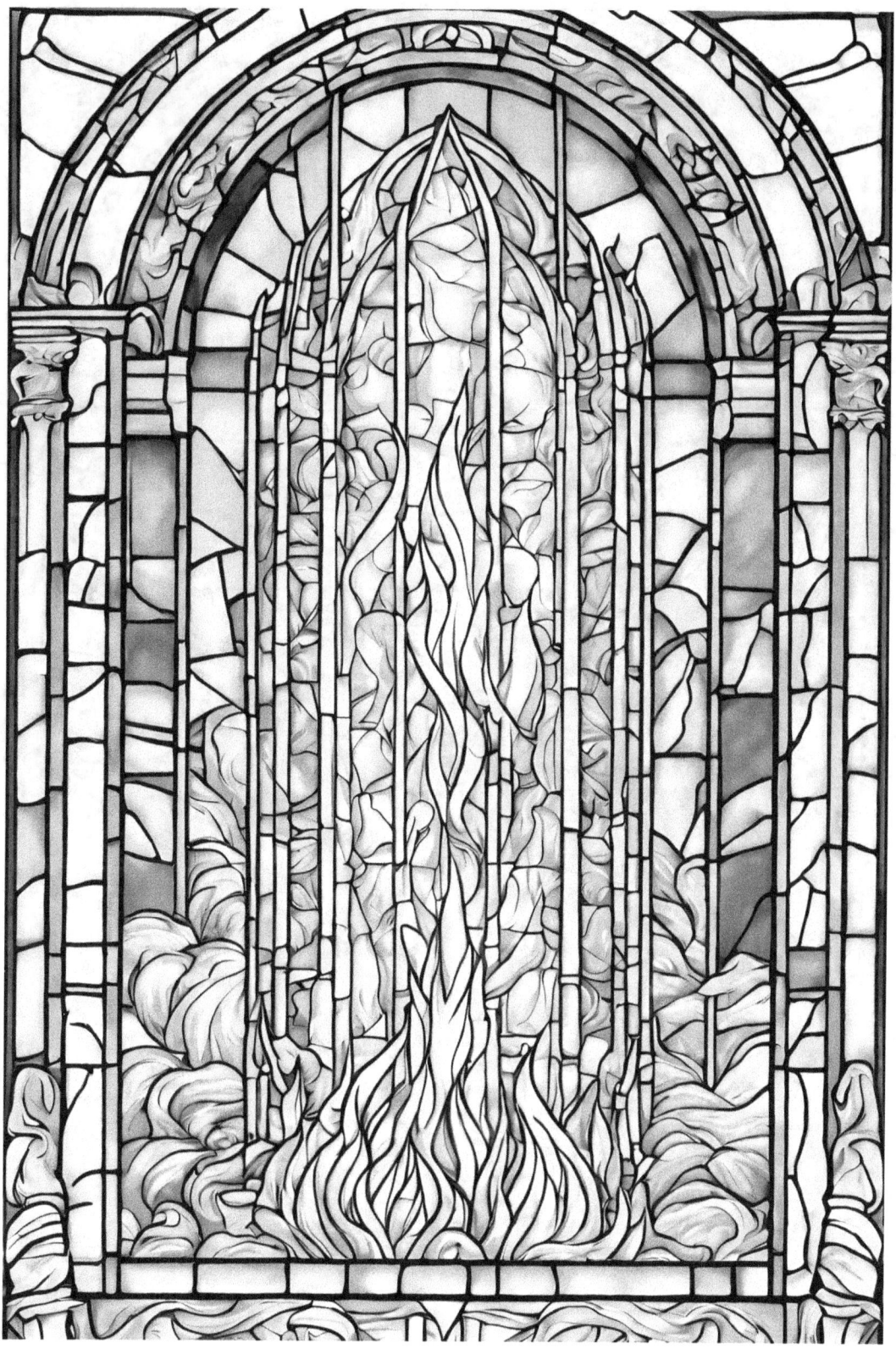

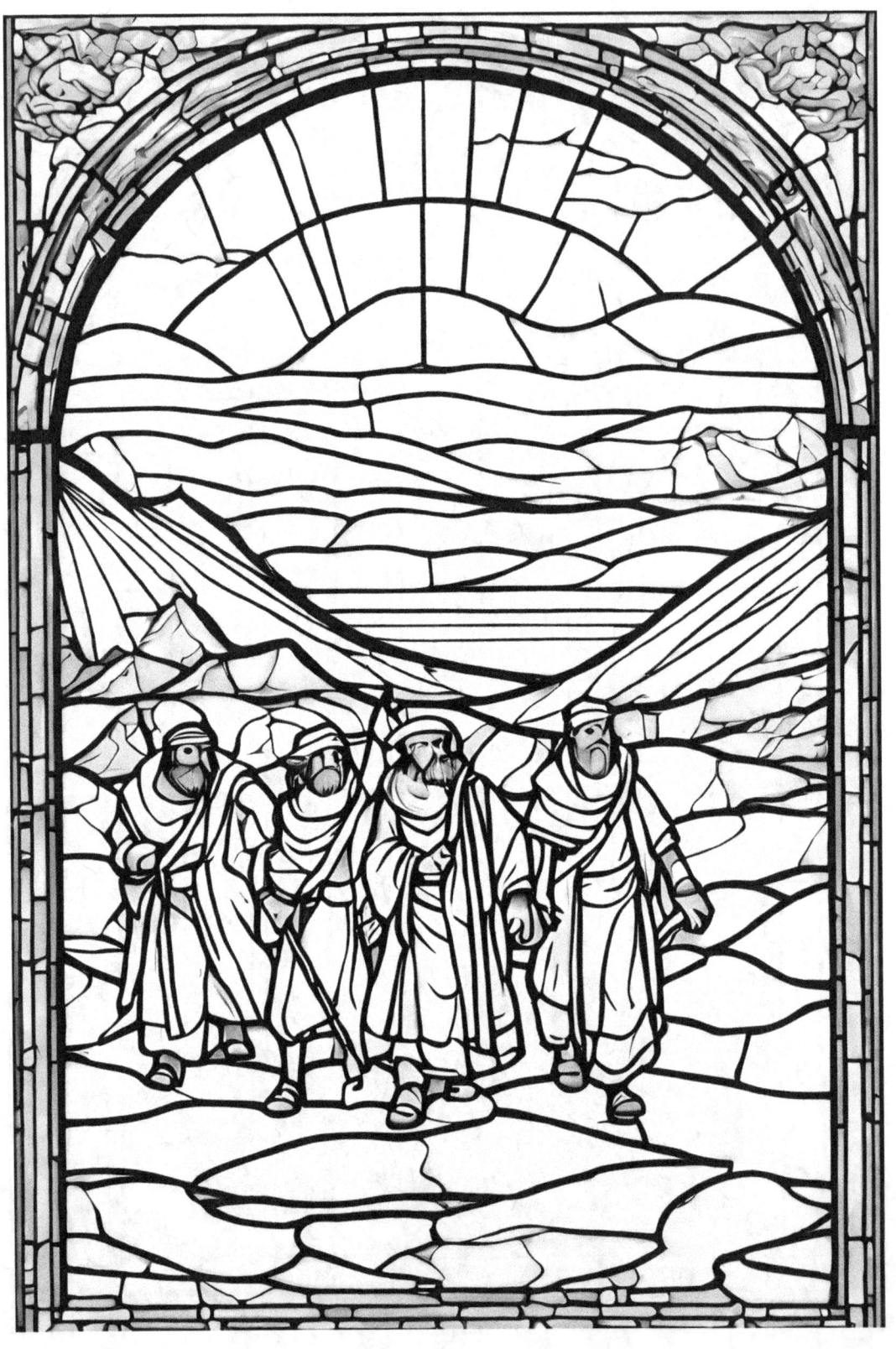

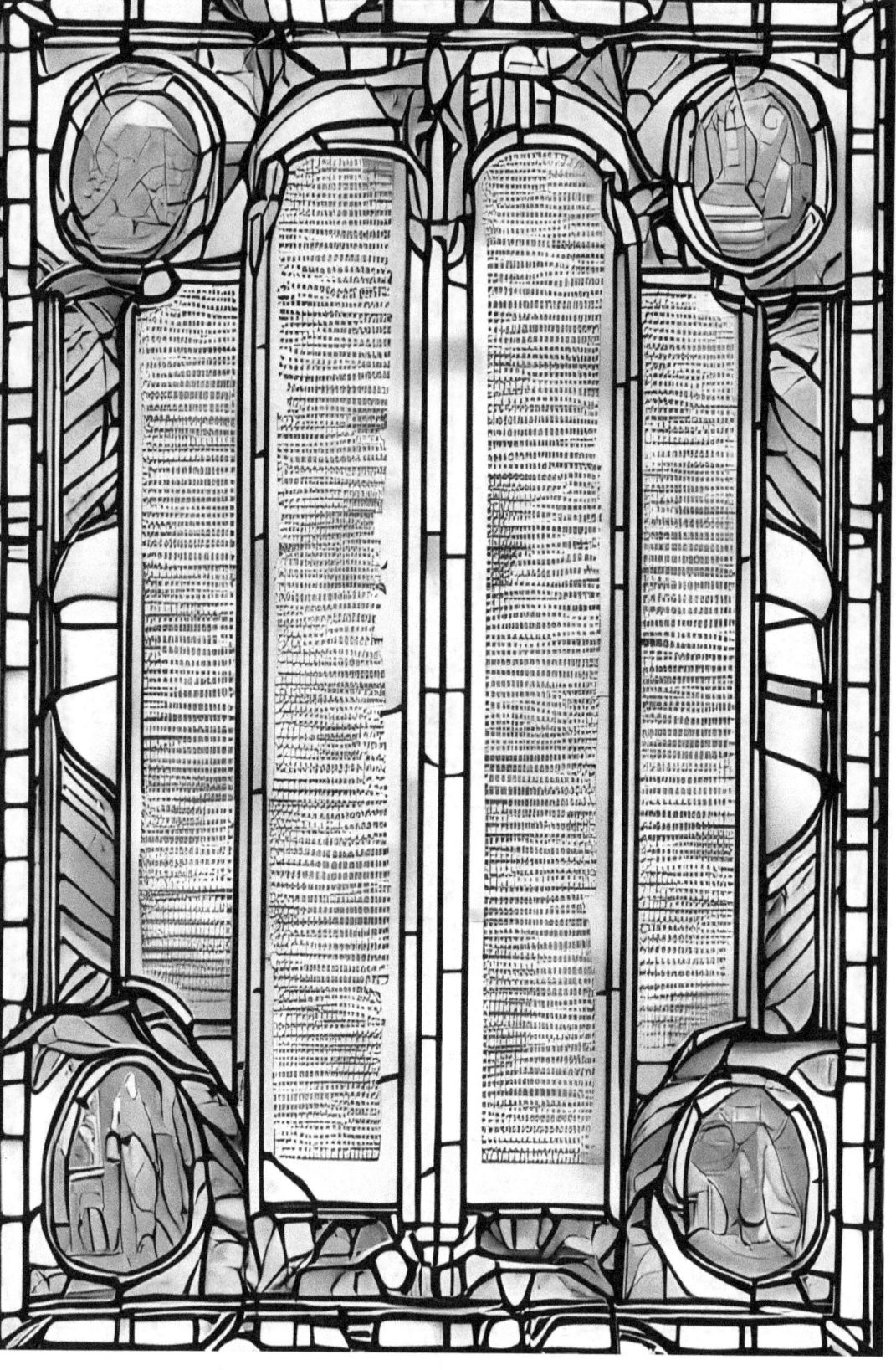

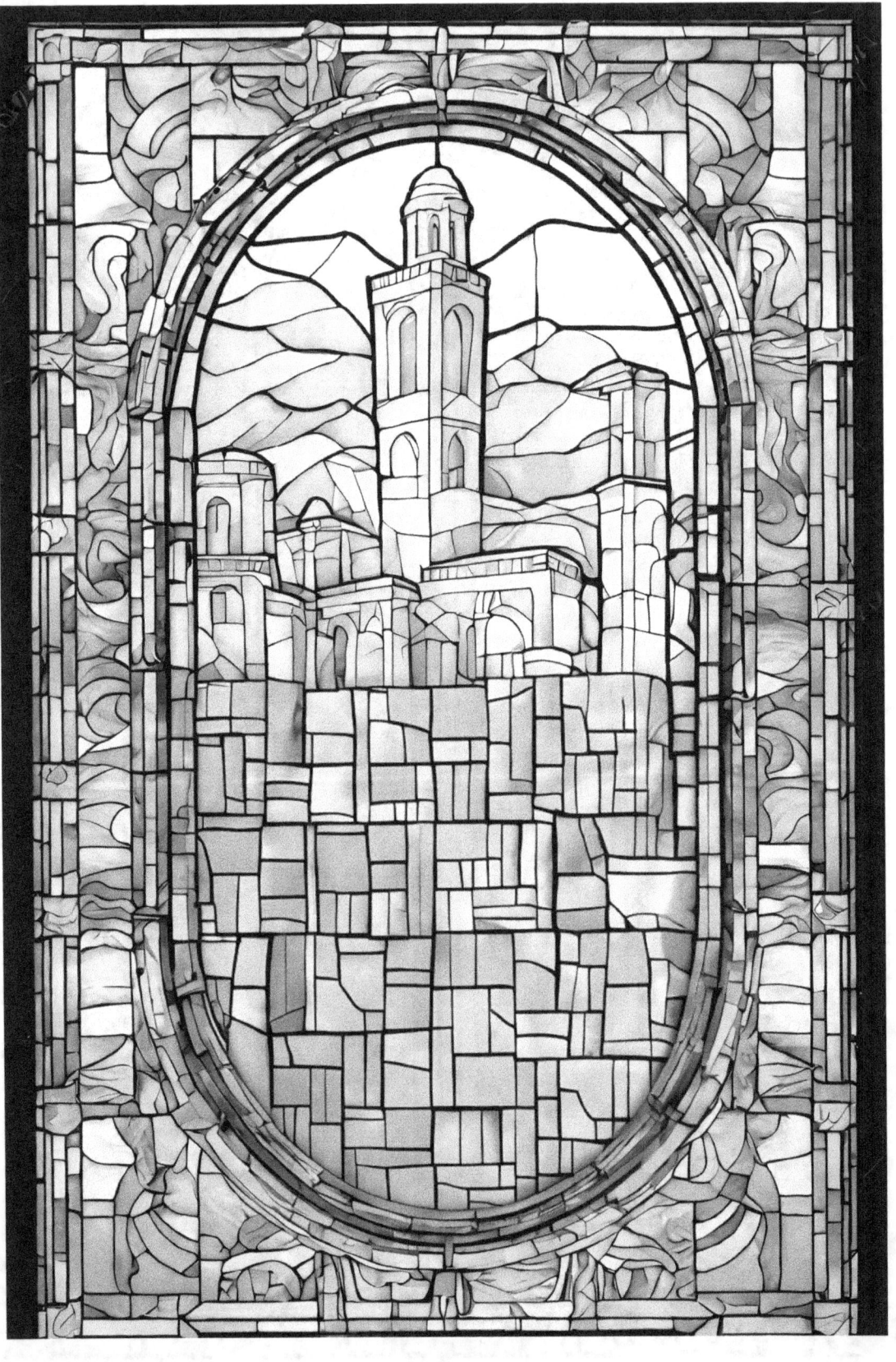

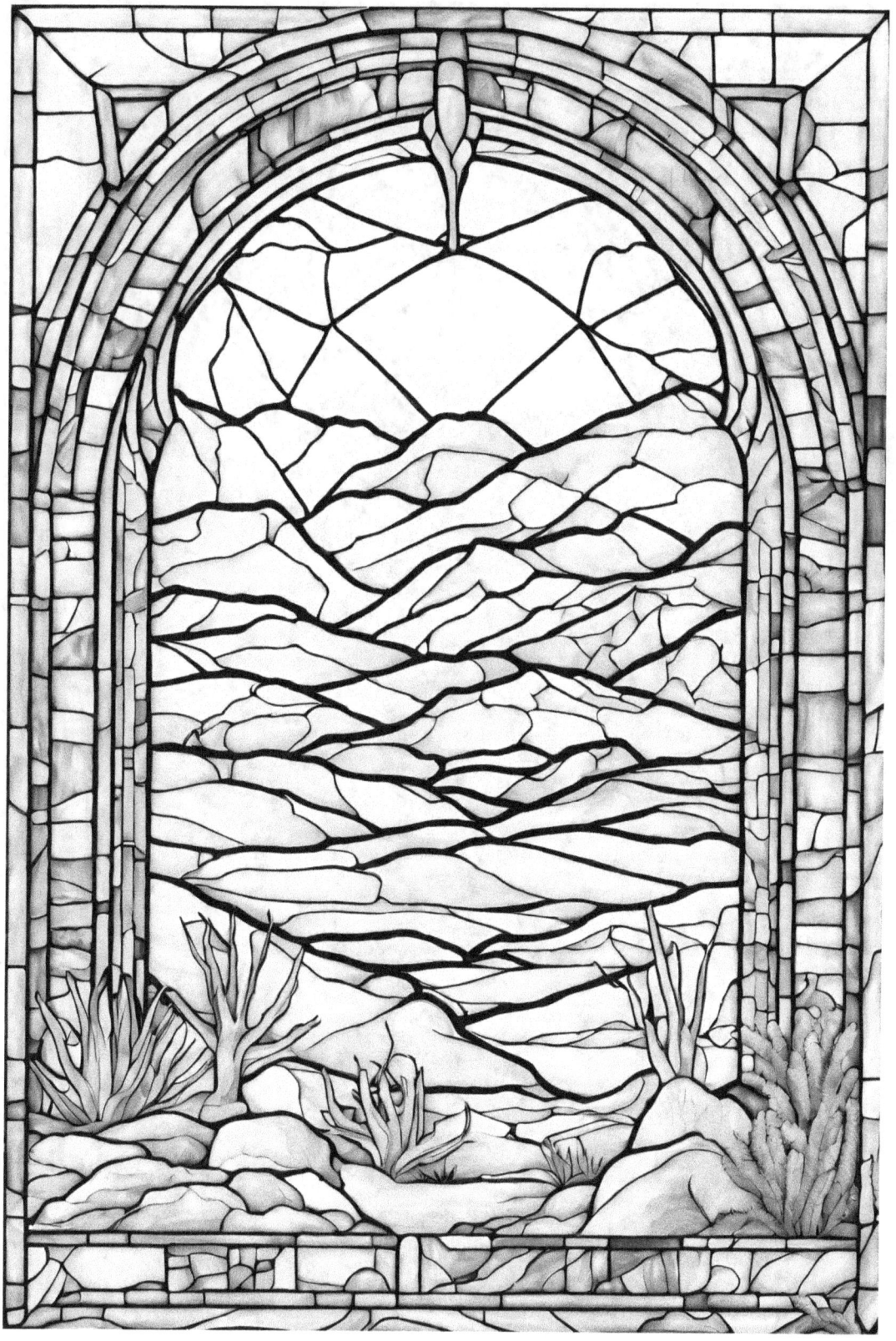

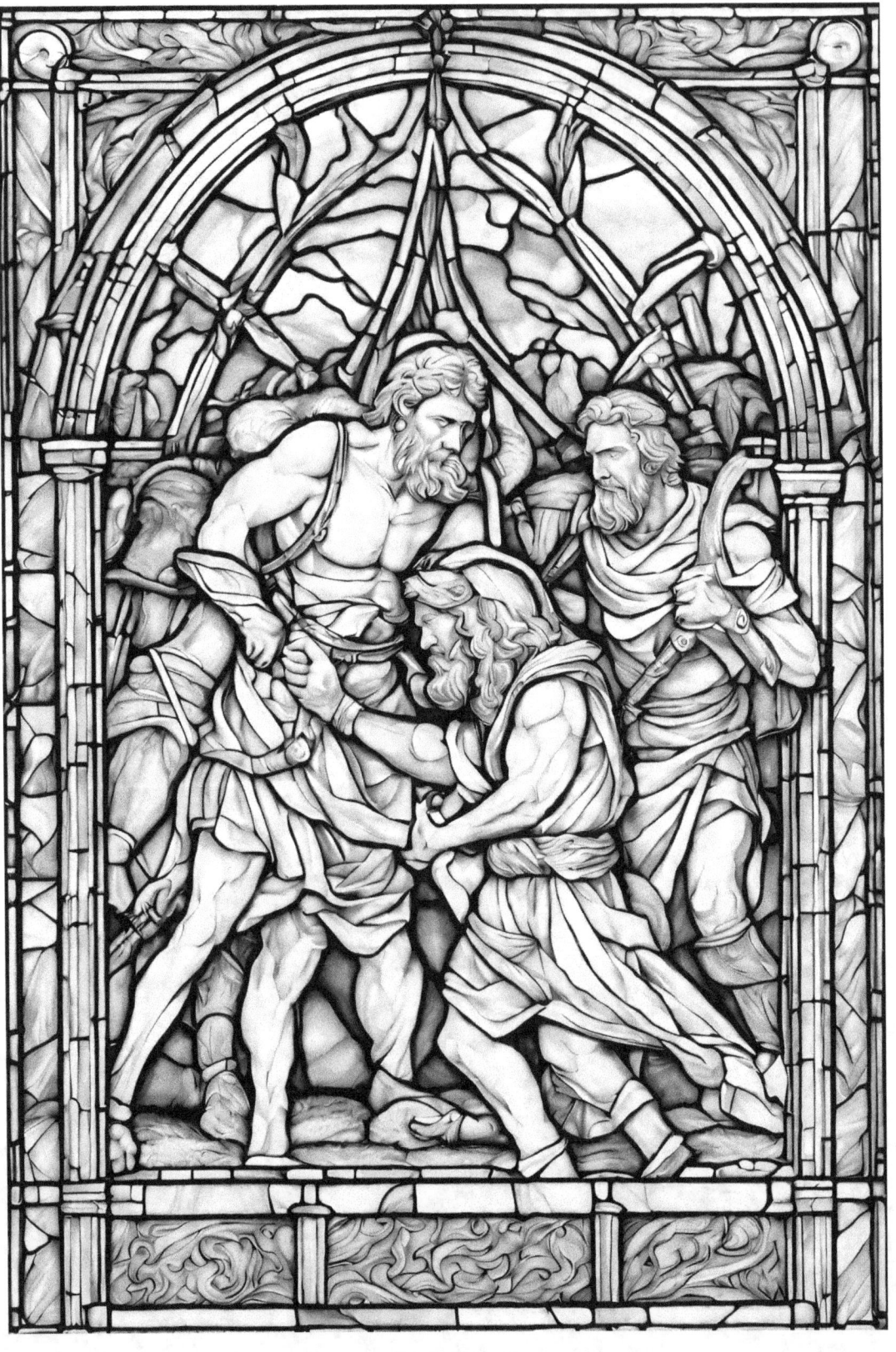

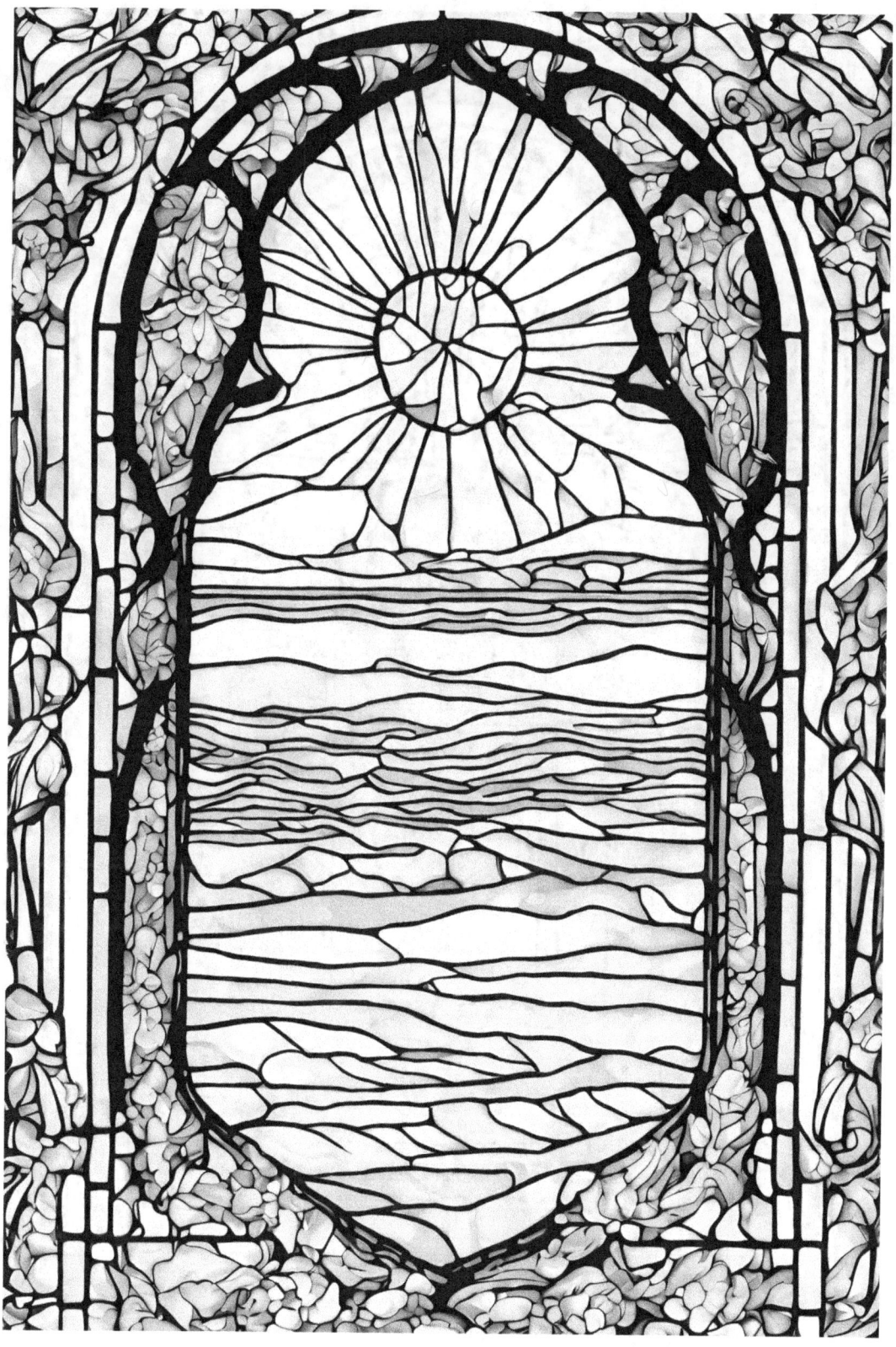

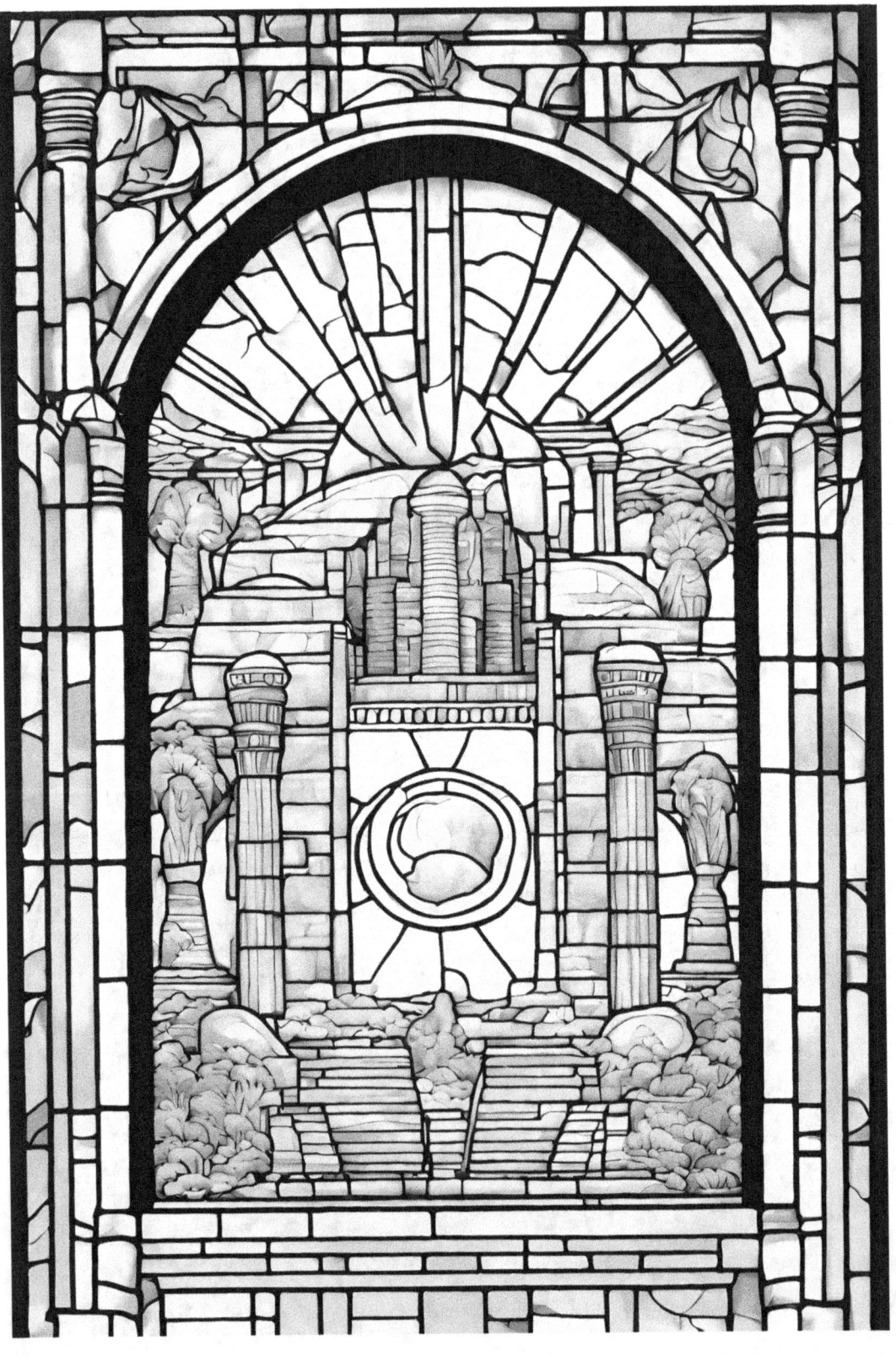

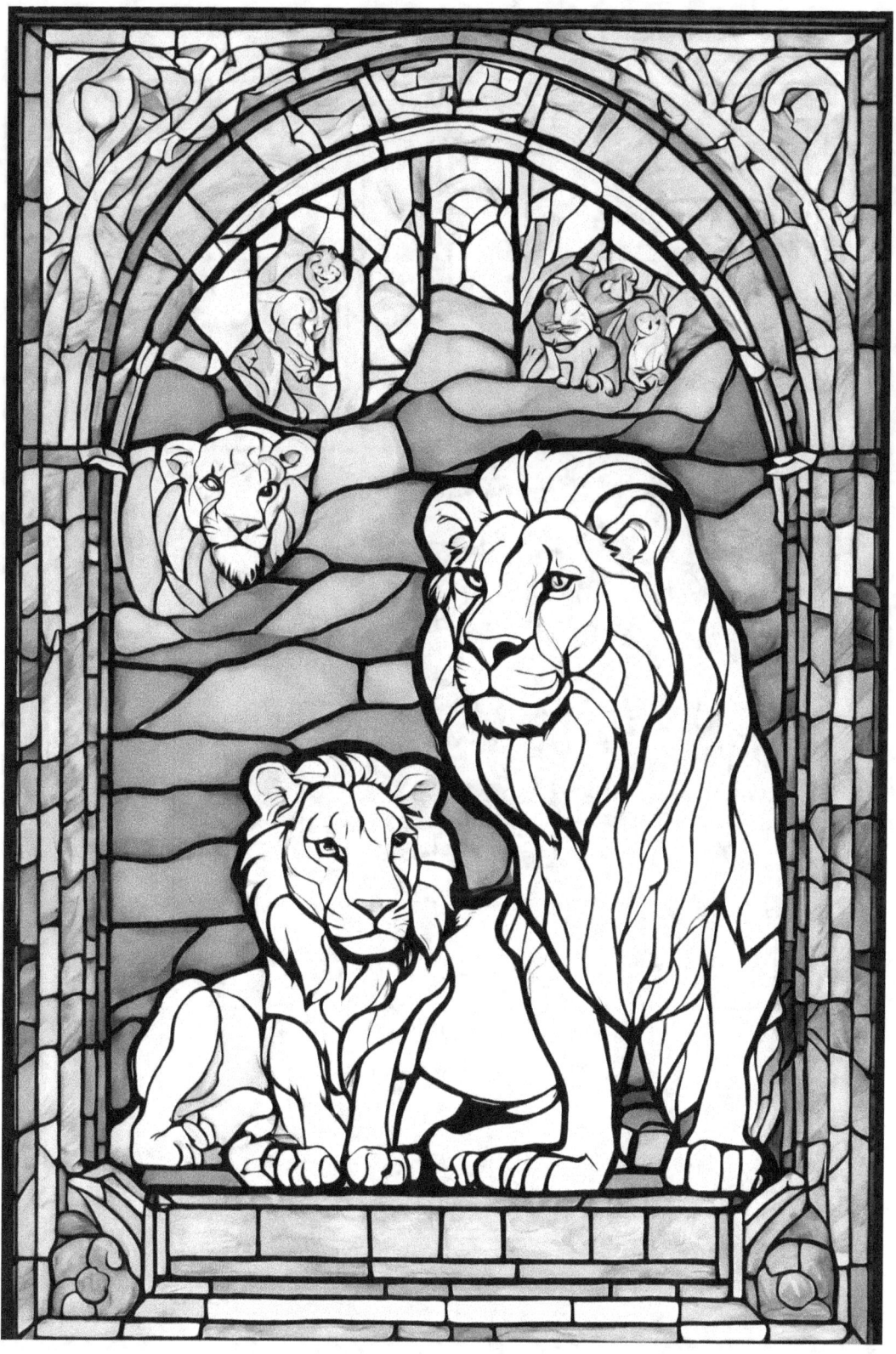

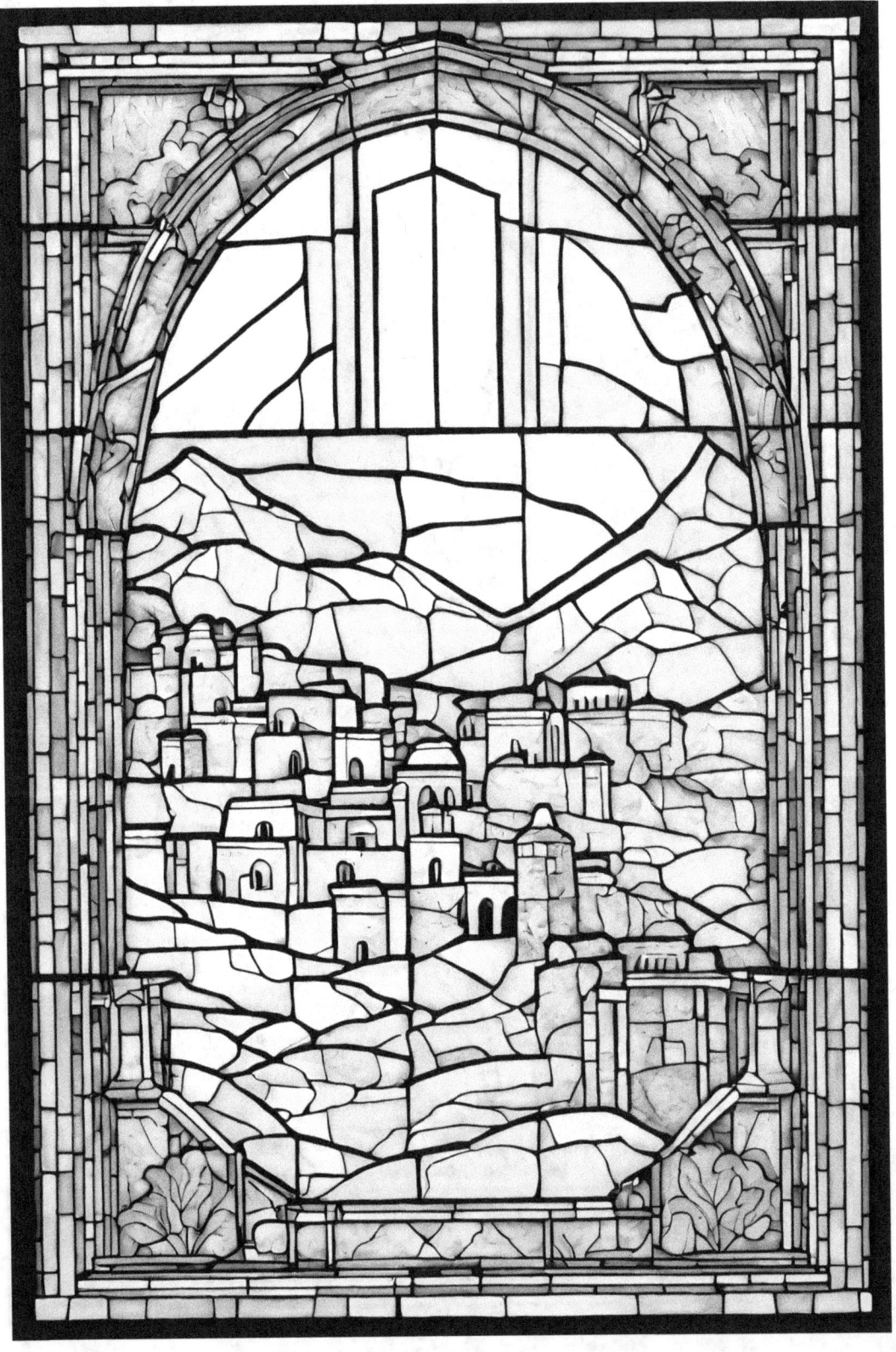

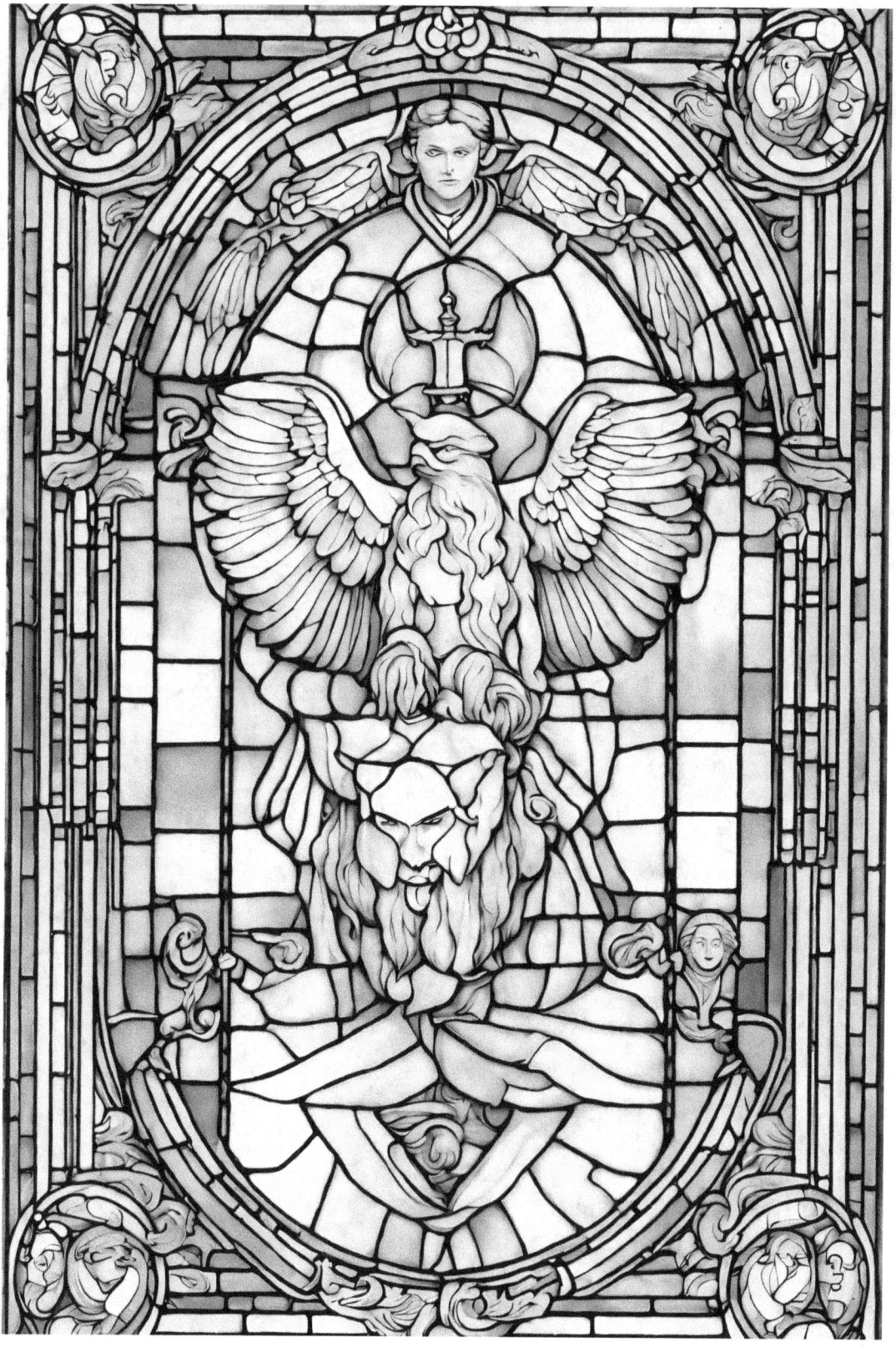

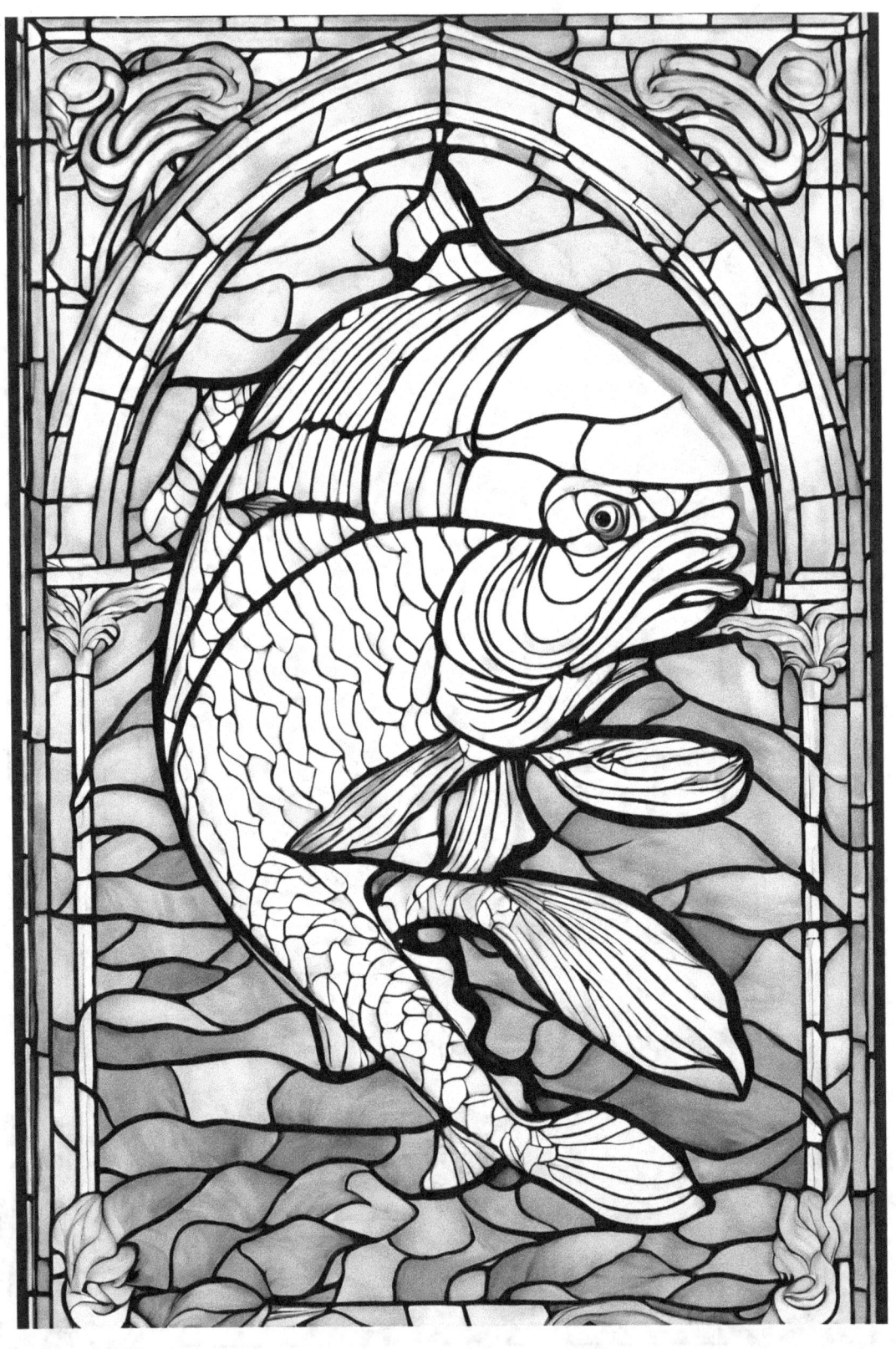

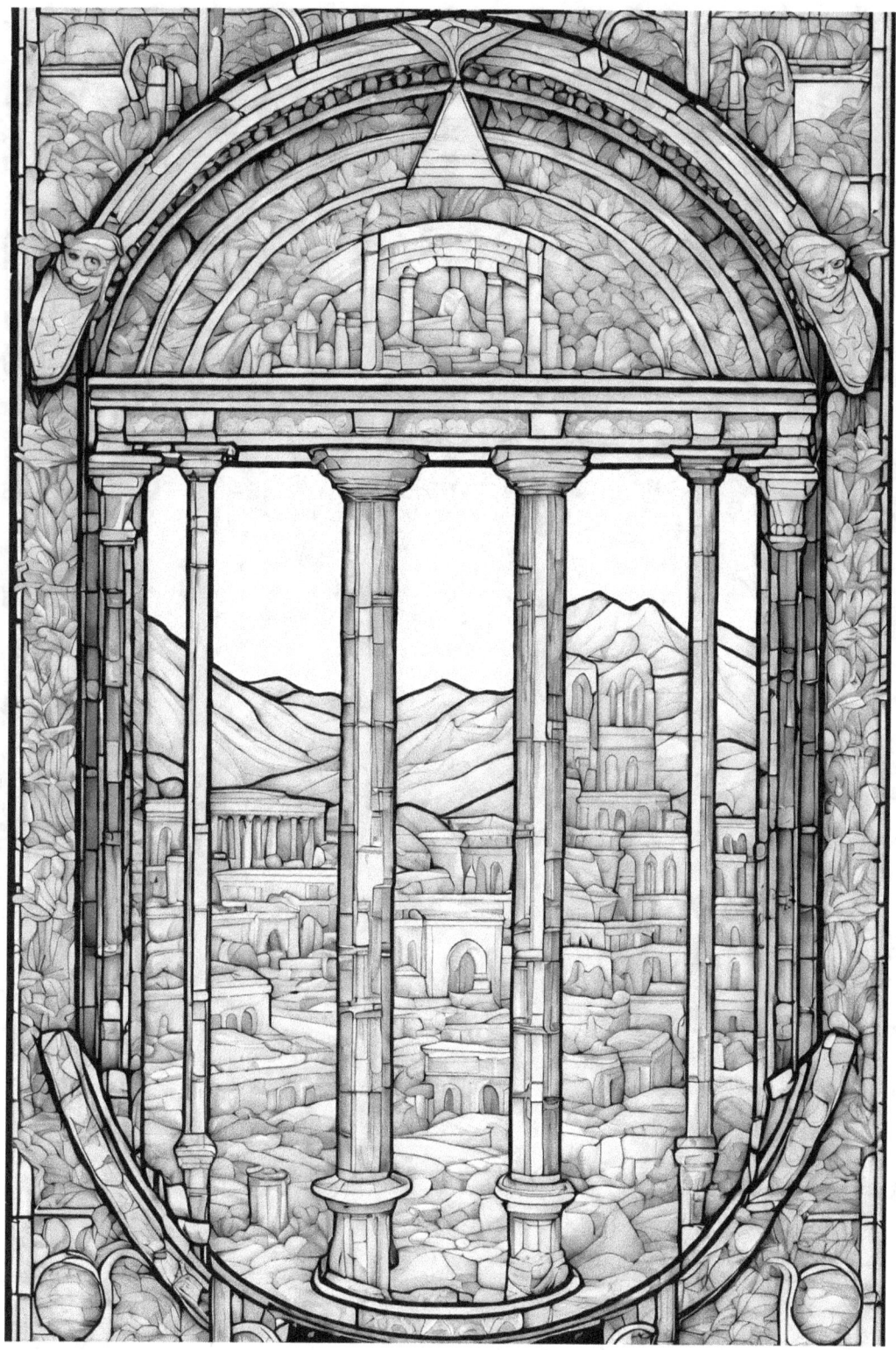

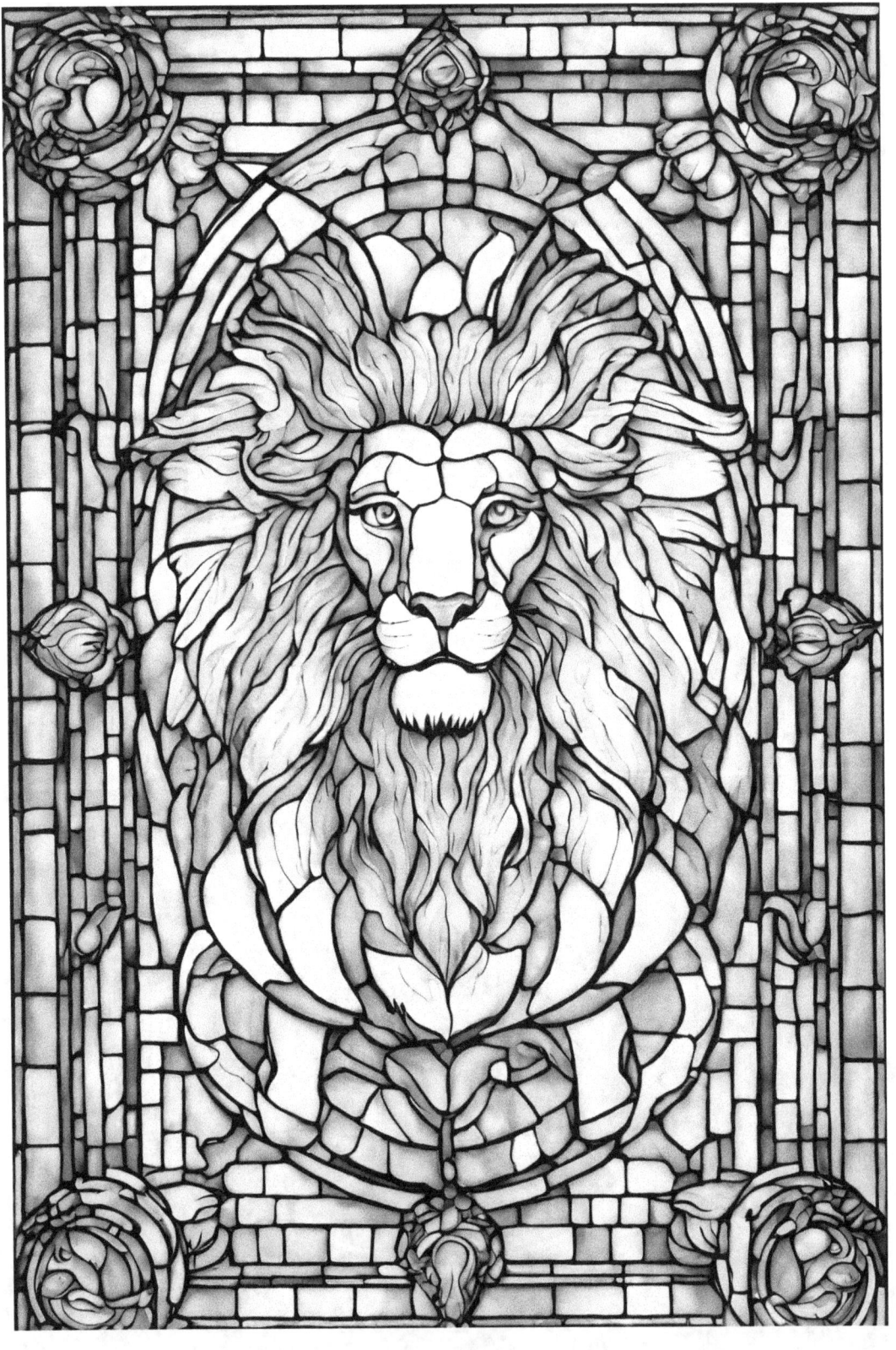

www.ingramcontent.com/pod-product-compliance
Lightning Source LLC
Chambersburg PA
CBHW081021240526
45471CB00018B/3930